Digital Citizenship

Digital Citizenship

Teaching Strategies and Practice from the Field

Carrie Rogers-Whitehead

ROWMAN & LITTLEFIELD
Lanham • Boulder • New York • London

Published by Rowman & Littlefield
An imprint of The Rowman & Littlefield Publishing Group, Inc.
4501 Forbes Boulevard, Suite 200, Lanham, Maryland 20706
www.rowman.com

6 Tinworth Street, London, SE11 5AL, United Kingdom

British Library Cataloguing in Publication Information Available

Library of Congress Cataloging-in-Publication Data

Names: Rogers-Whitehead, Carrie, 1983– author.
Title: Digital citizenship : teaching strategies and practice from the field / Carrie Rogers-Whitehead.
Description: Lanham, Maryland : Rowman & Littlefield, [2019] | Includes bibliographical references and index.
Identifiers: LCCN 2019010165 (print) | LCCN 2019018716 (ebook) | ISBN 9781475848274 (Electronic) | ISBN 9781475848250 (cloth : alk. paper) | ISBN 9781475848267 (pbk. : alk. paper)
Subjects: LCSH: Citizenship—Study and teaching—United States. | Digital media—Study and teaching—United States. | Media literacy—Study and teaching—United States. | Political participation—Technological innovations—United States. | Information society—United States.
Classification: LCC LC1091 (ebook) | LCC LC1091 .R73 2019 (print) | DDC 323.6071--dc23
LC record available at https://lccn.loc.gov/2019010165

To my husband, Kristopher.
You've been a support to our family to make this book happen.

Contents

Preface

I was a public librarian for eight years in a busy and diverse library west of Salt Lake City. The library was surrounded by Title 1 schools. A high school, junior high, and two elementary schools were all within walking distance. About 2:45 p.m. every day a stream of students would fill up our branch. It was the library staff's job to mentor, discipline, entertain, educate, and be there for these 100–150 kids, who would often stay until we closed at 9 p.m.

In library school they don't teach you how to defuse a fight, know when to call child protective services, how to calm a crying teen whose boyfriend just broke up with her, or monitor and report cyberbullying. I had to learn all that on the job. And in that learning and daily interactions, conversations, and work with children of all ages I learned how to listen better and how the impacts of their neighborhood, families, mental health, and more affected their attitudes and behaviors. I discovered that teens weren't necessarily "angsty" or "angry," they were tired and stressed. And I learned that there were gaps in education and how we understand and teach students.

A big gap I saw was in STEM education. I ran STEM afterschool programs for years and feel strongly that it's an important part of learning and a potential path out of poverty. However, I felt that the educational craze and hype around everything STEM masked a lacking.

STEM education is incomplete without addressing the *Whys? Why* are we adopting tech in schools and our homes? Is it better or just new? *Why* is it important to develop STEM skills? Is it for job security or something else? *Why* do we, even in this twenty-first century, with all this knowledge and tech, behave the way we do?

It was the search for answers for those *Whys* that led me to digital citizenship. I was a practitioner of digital citizenship at the library in my STEM programs, educating about protecting privacy, teaching information literacy and research skills, and handling cyberbullying for years before I heard the term "digital citizenship." When I discovered this whole new area of study it was like running into a childhood friend.

In 2015, I started preparing for that next step, to fill those gaps and make a difference in digital behavior. By the fall of the next year I was prepared to make that leap; I left that librarian job I enjoyed for the unknown. I founded Digital Respons-Ability to teach digital citizenship to students, and we quickly expanded that teaching to educators and parents.

I took all my knowledge, and relied on the knowledge of experts before me, to craft something new in digital citizenship. I wanted to focus on the entire person, and all of digital citizenship, not just online safety. This curriculum used teaching models I had found success in during those years of STEM programs, which are covered in chapter 4. The curriculum and teaching models are threaded with the principles of prevention science. These principles, covered extensively in chapter 2, informed all the teaching. I learned from years of working with adolescents that you don't *tell,* you *show* or *guide.* Along with a foundation in prevention science and teaching models, the first half of the book will catch you up on the discipline of digital citizenship (chapter 1), current and near-future tech trends (chapter 5), and strategies for assessing digital citizenship knowledge (chapter 2).

The teachings and practices in this book rely on firsthand experience, student input, provider/educator feedback of our programs, and the interviews and words of experts in the field. Yes, I have the degrees, but I have never been and do not consider myself an academic. I regularly teach digital citizenship along with my staff. I am out in the field and talking to teachers, parents, and students. Library school only prepared me part of the way for being a librarian. And talking or researching about digital citizenship will only prepare you part of the way for teaching it.

That direct input goes into the second half of the book, chapters 6–9. These chapters cover digital communication, media literacy, online safety, digital health, digital commerce, digital law, digital rights, and online privacy. Chapter 10 focuses on adapting that teaching to special populations. Digital Respons-Ability has worked with refugees and immigrants, students in custody, and individuals with disabilities, and we bring our experiences to that chapter to help educators make their digital citizenship work more inclusive. There are lesson plans scattered throughout the book along with original research. The appendixes have worksheets and other resources that can be copied and used to support the lessons and organizational digital citizenship initiatives.

Curriculum is never truly finished, and I continue to adapt it with different populations and as we teach it. Curriculum development is demanding and time-consuming work; evaluating, adding, editing, and more. But I'm happy with the result. Digital Respons-Ability has worked with hundreds of K–12 students to teach digital citizenship and we've found that students increase their knowledge and attitudes toward digital citizenship principles and show an increase in STEM careers after taking the program.

I hope that other educators can benefit from our work, just like I have benefited from others' research. Digital citizenship is a growing, multidisciplinary subject with a need for more practitioners. Help me address those gaps and the *Whys* through the practice of digital citizenship.

1

Current State of Digital Citizenship

When I walked into Twitter headquarters for the second annual Digital Citizenship Summit, people were vibrating with energy. There was a feeling of excitement and enthusiasm among the attendees. The Twitter staff was friendly and busy sharing coffee and food. Selfies were taken, and there were many, many tweets. I could feel the enthusiasm, but as I looked around the room my thoughts returned not to who was in the room, but who wasn't. On a subject like digital citizenship, that affects so many people, Twitter headquarters should have been standing room only.

—*Story from the author*

When compared to disciplines such as education, computer science, librarianship, and engineering, digital citizenship is a newborn baby. This is exciting; there's a feeling of energy from practitioners and participants like at the second annual Digital Citizenship Summit. But it also means there's a lack of unified vision and data. To understand how to teach digital citizenship, educators must understand where it's been, where it is now, and where it's going.

HISTORY OF DIGITAL CITIZENSHIP

Like most movements in history, there was not one person or one organization that "started" digital citizenship. It arose from the ground up through educators, academics, and others who were seeing the effects of technology on their students.

The focus of digital citizenship in its early years versus the present has shifted. There is not an exact date that the digital citizenship movement started, but the words started appearing in the larger media in the late 1990s as more technology came into classrooms. During that time, there was a focus on access. You cannot be a digital citizen if you do not have access to the internet or devices to connect online.

Pew Research started tracking Internet usage of Americans in 2000 when half of adults were online. That number has increased to 90 percent of adults in 2018. Two-thirds of American homes have broadband internet service, while that number was close to zero in 2000.

There are still issues with access, and it is a part of digital citizenship. To use the analogy of Maslow's hierarchy of needs, access is at the bottom of the digital citizenship pyramid. People must have access needs met before they can focus on other areas of digital citizenship. However, many of the conversations of access have moved from educators to policy makers and tech companies.

Another focus of digital citizenship in the early stages was the word *citizen*. The first city in the United States to make a digital inclusion plan was Seattle. City officials realized that individuals could not be fully participating citizens if they could not access the internet. With taxes, community information, registration for various public services, and more being moved online, the argument that individuals had a constitutional right to access the internet was made.

In 1995 Seattle unveiled its digital inclusion plan, and it continues to make digital equity a focus of the city. Their website on digital equity states, "Seattle is working together for digital equity, to ensure all residents and neighborhoods have the information technology capacity needed for civic and cultural participation, employment, lifelong learning, and access to essential services."

The word *citizen* was also related to an individual's relation to the economy, not only to democratic institutions. One definition of digital citizenship in the 2007 book *Digital Citizenship: The Internet, Society, and Participation* described it as "the ability to participate in society online" and attached that knowledge and access to economic prosperity. The research conducted in *Digital Citizenship: The Internet, Society, and Participation* stated, "Our findings provide powerful evidence that digital citizenship matters for economic participation and technology disparities are not a trivial concern for future equality of opportunity." Individuals working in the knowledge economy have higher wages, which creates divides between other sectors. "The growth of income inequality through the development of the new economy is in part the result of fundamental technological change that has increased the need for information technology skills."

There are continuing conversations of students being digital citizens for economic and political reasons. However, that knowledge is now mostly a given. Educators, academics, government officials, and students almost universally agree that individuals should have access and the literacy skills to participate in their government and to find and secure jobs. Agreement does not always result in action, and disparities in access and skills are stark. But the digital citizenship movement has less focus on those external, societal goals, and now looks more at the internal.

Where Is Digital Citizenship Now?

The conversation around digital citizenship continues to evolve and shift. Nancy Watson is an Instructional Technology Specialist and has been involved since the beginning with the digital citizenship movement (abbreviated to digcit).

> I've seen the conversation about digcit grow from a list of "don'ts" and equating digcit with not cyberbullying among people who talk about digcit. The focus is moving from the fear and risk narrative to a more positive narrative of empowerment and opportunity. People new to the conversation often start at the "don't cyberbully" stage, but there are lot of resources out there to encourage educators to be more sophisticated in their thinking.

There continues to be feelings of fear, but a growing number of educators are pushing back and realizing that they need to be proactive rather than reactive. According to Watson, part of the reason more educators are talking about digital citizenship is the growth of technology in schools. "The prevalence of 1:1 devices plays a large part; educators simply can't ignore the need for digital citizenship instruction the way they may have been able to in the past." She adds, "I think one of the reasons social media has gotten so mean and nasty is that nobody has been teaching how to behave online! Now we are waking up to the fact that actively teaching students to be positive when they go online is the way to go."

There is also a move from the "hard" skills of technology like how to type, the mechanics of hardware, and what specifically must be done to get it to work. Those skills, while important and still taught, are becoming more of a given in recent years. There is an increasing focus on the application of technology, how to create, share, and know when to use it appropriately.

This shift can be seen in the International Society for Technology for Education's (ISTE) standards. The original *Technology Foundation Standards for Students* came in 1998. The original standards reference basic digital literacy skills: "Students demonstrate a sound understanding of the nature and operation of technology systems." The updated standards, which came out in 2016, are more about the application and use of technology, not just the understanding: "Students collect data or identify relevant data sets, use digital tools to analyze them, and represent data in various ways to facilitate problem-solving and decision-making."

Technology Foundation Standards for Students did not reference digital citizenship directly, but it takes note of "social ethical and human issues," recommending that "students develop positive attitudes toward technology uses that support lifelong learning, collaboration, personal pursuits, and productivity." The updated 2016 resource directly names digital citizenship with its own set of standards. The newer standards go further, referencing digital identity, intellectual property, digital privacy, and more.

CURRENT STATE OF DIGITAL CITIZENSHIP

At the third annual Digital Citizenship Summit I was sitting at a table with a non-profit professional, a college student, educational technology trainers and a business owner. All the tables were like that, a mix from many different industries. I liked the conversations we had, although even though there were conversations over two days, I didn't feel like there was enough!

—Story from the author

Who Is Involved in Digital Citizenship?

There is not one authoritative source and guide for digital citizenship in the world. It is a growing movement with a diverse set of perspectives, opinions, and work. The movement includes teachers, politicians, celebrities, journalists, religious authorities, marketing and public relations professionals, bureaucrats, librarians, students, academics, and more. Digital citizenship is such a multidisciplinary study that it affects many professions.

However, there are certain professions, people, and organizations that have played a longer and/or larger role in the movement. One profession in particular has been involved with digital citizenship before there were the words *digital citizenship*. Those are professionals in library science.

At the second annual Digital Citizenship Summit I asked jokingly on stage how many in the audience were former or current librarians. While this was certainly not a scientific poll, it was telling that many hands shot up.

Librarians have been involved in digital citizenship for several reasons. First, digital citizenship involves being able to navigate information, and librarians are specifically trained to be information literate and help people find resources. Next, the librarian position is sometimes the only one in a school that has specific Common Core or other education standards related to digital citizenship. Finally, librarians in the twenty-first century are increasingly involved in technology. Many librarians have their responsibilities split between traditional library work with books and acting as the technology specialist for the school. They are often troubleshooting, teaching, and implementing new technology in schools.

Another player in the digital citizenship movement has already been mentioned: ISTE. This nonprofit based in Portland, Oregon, creates standards and professional development and provides resources for those who work in educational technology in over one hundred countries around the globe. ISTE standards will be referenced multiple times in this book.

Common Sense Media, a nonprofit based in San Francisco, California, is also a leading resource around the subject of digital citizenship. It is particularly known for media reviews, but it also provides digital citizenship education.

In recent years, technology companies have been more involved in the digital citizenship movement. Whether this is an attempt to deflect the backlash with technology-related problems and scandals or a genuine interest in making change, or both, is unknown. However, large companies such as Twitter, Facebook, Google, Snapchat, Firefox, Instagram, and others are part of the conversation.

Elements of Digital Citizenship

Standards of digital citizenship have moved from skills in understanding and knowledge to ones of application and attitude. Students no longer have a weekly computer class, but technology is integrated in almost every subject. New students go into kindergarten with familiarity on devices, and school is typically no longer their first introduction to a computer. These shifts have required a new type of digital citizenship. The new standards of digital citizenship understand that technology is not a once-a-week discussion but an everyday occurrence, part of life from waking to sleeping.

Dr. Mike Ribble, author of *Digital Citizenship in Schools*, articulated these elements of digital citizenship with Gerard Bailey in the first edition of his book in 2007. The elements were later elaborated and defined in the second and third editions. When asked how those elements have evolved since the 2007 edition, Ribble

Figure 1.1. Author and Mike Ribble at the third annual National DigCit Summit. *Courtesy of the author*

said, "Much of the focus in the early years was on the negative side of technology. Many wanted to have a list of things not to do online. We still need to assist new users on the pitfalls when using technology [but] there is now more of a focus of what are the possibilities when interacting online without losing focus on those that are around us."

The updated nine elements include:

1. Digital access
2. Digital commerce
3. Digital communication
4. Digital literacy
5. Digital etiquette
6. Digital law
7. Digital rights and responsibilities
8. Digital health and wellness
9. Digital safety and security

These elements will be detailed in later chapters along with curricula, strategies, and research and experience from teaching them in the field. To be a full and participating digital citizen, a holistic approach must be used. Ribble said, "Often we focus on some aspects more frequently, like communication and etiquette, but there is a need for all the elements to be a productive member of a community." If technology surrounds and affects multiple parts of our lives, then our education around that technology must cover all those parts.

National Digital Citizenship Summit

As noted, there are many players in the digital citizenship space. It's a subject that crosses disciplines. With the many, sometimes competing, voices, there are efforts to bring consensus and collaboration. One large effort is the Digital Citizenship Summit (DigCitSummit) hosted by the Digital Citizenship Institute. The Institute describes the summits as "a gathering of digital citizenship enthusiasts and influencers from around the world. The DigCitSummit builds connections among four critical stakeholders namely, students, educators, parents and business leaders."

Figure 1.2. Logo of the National DigCitSummit. ***National Digital Citizenship Institute***

The DigCitSummit started as a small, regional event in 2015 in Connecticut. The next year the event happened San Francisco at Twitter headquarters. In the third year, the summit began to expand more into international space, with one larger event and smaller regional events. The third annual DigCitSummit was in Utah, with other events in Spain and Mexico. In 2018, the event was held in St. Louis, and other events continue to grow in such countries as Canada and Ireland.

In addition to the DigCitSummit, there are other efforts to spread awareness and advocacy for digital citizenship. In 2017, the nonprofit #ICANHELP started hosting a student-centered summit called #Digital4Good. Common Sense Media celebrates a digital citizenship week each October. Individual school districts and other organizations also host digital citizenship events. In 2019, the fifth annual National DigCit Summit will be completely online for a week in partnership with EduMatch.

Many communities and individuals are needed to make the shift in culture, norms, and conversation. Michelle Linford, one of the organizers of the third annual National Digital Citizenship Summit, said that what is needed is "educators and parents and people from all sectors working together and having continuous conversations. . . . We can't adapt to the world if we work alone in pods and pockets of expertise or focus."

Gaps in Digital Citizenship

In April 2017, I attended a leadership council in preparation for the third annual DigCitSummit in Utah that fall. The event was very collaborative, with only a few talks and the rest of the work done in small, facilitated groups. In one brainstorming session, I remember the participants would put up Post-it notes about what digital citizenship meant to them. Some people had over a dozen notes that they would add to a wall of butcher paper. Some people would call out a specific element like "media literacy" or "being kind online."

Then one guest from Africa quietly stood up with only one Post-it. Written on the Post-it was only one word: "Access." He stuck it on the paper and described how in his country this was the most important thing; that access affected everything else and that you couldn't have digital citizenship without it. The group was quiet for a second; access hadn't even been mentioned in all those dozens of colorful notes posted on the wall. That brainstorming session stuck with me more than anything during the leadership council. It taught that digital citizenship impacts people in widely different ways.

—Story from the author

Collaboration efforts in digital citizenship are needed because there are large gaps. One missing piece in the many different perspectives and practices is a unifying vision. There are strong opinions about the positives of technology, and the negatives—both in the same room. For those in countries with limited technology, there is less concern about such subjects as media literacy than about basic tools to access the internet.

Dr. Ribble said, "I would agree that there are gaps in demographics receiving digital citizenship. Since education is heavily a [local] (community-based) institution, these are the choices that they are making." Digital citizenship can be considered an "add-on" or even a luxury in schools that do not have the infrastructure to support many devices or that have limited staff. Other school structures, like a juvenile detention facility, provide no or very limited technology access due to safety concerns. Digital citizenship education, like digital access, is not spread equally across geography or demographics. This subject of teaching digital citizenship to special populations will be explored more in chapter 10.

The approach for digital citizenship education has typically been from teacher to student, but who trains the teacher? Dr. Ribble describes his experiences: "I teach a course in a Master's program for educators that are interested in integrating technology in their classroom. I have teachers from various stages in their careers from first few years to 20+ years. . . . There are so many programs in schools today that there is not enough time to cover their Professional Learning [let] alone adding technology instruction and discussion."

Another gap is in research. The smartphone has only been popularized since the release of the iPhone in 2007. Social media have only been around for approximately the same time. We have little understanding of the long-term effects of technology, since not enough time has passed. There is a research gap because of the lack of studies in this area.

There is more talking than doing in digital citizenship. It is simpler to talk about the dangers of cyberbullying than to develop, test, and evaluate curricula to deal with it. Changing outcomes takes time, patience, and highly trained practitioners. Throughout this book data from original research will be shared to help fill in the gaps.

Digital citizenship lessons are typically one-offs and not integrated in the classroom on a regular basis or reinforced at home. It is difficult to grasp the effectiveness of teaching by such short-term methods, particularly if there are no evaluation tools. What is studied is also incomplete. Surveys and studies typically focus more on online safety and communication than on addressing all nine elements of digital citizenship. "For some the research has always been on the outcomes of inappropriate technology use (i.e., cyberbullying, sexting, etc.)," said Ribble. "We need to get to the reasons why people use technology inappropriately." This is where using a prevention science framework is needed, which will be explored in depth in chapter 2.

FUTURE OF DIGITAL CITIZENSHIP

What is the future of digital citizenship? That's a question that's hard to answer. Technology continues to change rapidly with new iterations of devices, apps springing up left and right, and faster speeds and easier access. And more and more screens are found in homes and schools. These technology trends will be explored in further detail in chapter 5.

Societal changes also keep up a fast pace. Most of Generation Z, those born around the mid-1990s, have used the internet since they were young, and the generation right behind, the Alphas, have had their lives documented online since they were in the womb. What are the long-term implications of children growing up in such a world, a world that's completely different from the rest of human history? What will be the new norms created in this world? And will digital citizenship become a basic part of education, like a math or English class?

Mike Ribble said,

> These new tools are moving us as people to connect differently, both personally and professionally. We are still learning how to balance who we are online as well as face-to-face. There are some that see this new interaction with digital devices will become the new norm and the term "digital" will be dropped. I can see us moving in this direction but there will need to be more of an understanding of how we act/react with technology before we drop the digital.

The digital citizenship movement has changed quickly since its first incarnation, with adjusted standards, more awareness, a larger professional network, and the beginnings of change in public policy. Ribble, who has seen the movement from its infancy, said, "There were many years that I was not sure there was interest in digital citizenship. . . . It has been great to see where we were and what are some of the possibilities in the future."

The future of digital citizenship will increasingly involve students and the community. In its early history, it was defined by academics and technology specialists. Students are more involved in the discussion and increasingly the student voice (#stuvoice) is heard. Technology gives the opportunities for students to speak out and be more involved. The younger generation, who have used the internet since they began to talk, can provide important perspectives for adults.

Norms are shifting, and teachers have an important part in creating those norms for the younger generation. When asked what she saw as the future of digital citizenship, Nancy Watson said,

> My fondest desire is that teachers would collectively develop an online culture of positive norms. I always point to the examples of smoking in restaurants or the Keep America Beautiful campaign as ways that cultural norms have changed over time. Although legislation is responsible in some measure for the fact that our public spaces are now largely smoking-free zones and we no longer litter the way we once did, it's also because public opinion can change. . . . I believe that we can make "positive" and "encouraging" the agreed-upon norms.

2

Human Behavior Is the Core of Digital Citizenship

"I just don't get it," the foster parent said, "we've been trying everything. He can't have a phone, we limit computer time in the house, but he keeps talking to his old friends. He knows *they're bad news, they're part of the reason he's here, but he refuses to stop. We've discussed this and taken all the tech, but it's not doing anything. I don't know what to do."*

Parents and educators may sometimes feel at the end of their rope. They've clearly communicated house rules or school policies, they've limited the tech, they've explained the problem, but it doesn't seem to do anything. The device comes out surreptitiously from underneath a pillow or hides behind an open book. And when confronted, denial or anger is often the result. This scenario plays out daily in homes and classrooms. Bans, limits, and other methods don't seem to change the behavior.

"He won't stop playing video games."
"She won't go to sleep. She keeps texting her friends."
"Her friends keep messing with her online, but she won't stop talking to them."
"I never see her, she's in her room all the time with her phone."
"He's just angry all the time."
"She's sending nudes to her boyfriend. I raised her better than that."

Why does this behavior occur? And why does banning and limiting devices not seem to help? The answer lies beyond the screen.

STRONG FEELINGS AROUND TECHNOLOGY

The author has been teaching digital citizenship principles to a cohort with the University of Utah. The university started a pilot program in 2017, partnering with a national nonprofit, First Star Academy. Research by Dr. Kathleen Reardon inspires First Star's work. Reardon's research finds that only about 3 percent of youth in foster care go on to attend a university. First Star partners with school districts, universities, nonprofits, and other organizations to help them transition to higher education and adulthood.

With teens in foster care, extremes both in teen and parent behavior around technology are evident. According to the US Department of Health and Human Services, the number one reason a child is removed from the home is due to neglect. Teens going into foster care have had less parental supervision than their peers and typically have little or no restrictions or communication around technology. These youth, raised in homes with few rules or guidance, move into homes where the foster parents are particularly concerned around technology. The parents are required to have hours of training from the state to be licensed as foster parents, but that training typically is not around technology. Foster parents, particularly those with teens, have experienced some of the negatives around technology. And there are negatives, particularly with vulnerable youth in foster care. Some things that could happen are:

- A biological family member finds the teen on social media and is a negative influence.
- A teen continues to talk to old friends in their past home who participate in illegal activities.
- A biological mother or father asks the teen for money.
- A teen finds a boyfriend or girlfriend online, who asks them to do things they are uncomfortable with, like exchanging sexual photos.

The foster parents have legitimate concerns and fears around technology. And the teens have legitimate needs for a social outlet and freedom. Finding a balance between safety and autonomy is difficult, particularly when emotions are high.

Sometimes adults go into bigger extremes. Go to YouTube and you can find dozens of videos of parents hammering, crushing, and destroying video game consoles and phones. One viral video, "Psycho Dad Destroys Xbox," starts with the father tossing his son's Xbox in the fireplace. Visibly upset and yelling, the son reaches into the fire to retrieve it, risking injury. The father wordlessly takes the singed console and smashes it onto the ground outside, the son horribly screaming the entire time. The brother, who is filming the event, laughs to himself.

The video is hard to watch, and one feels sympathetic to both the father and the son. How did they get to that place? What led them to it? And what could be done to prevent it?

Reflection: Think about the YouTube video "Psycho Dad Destroys Xbox" through a prevention science model. Go beyond the screen to the father and son's motivations.

- Was the son playing with friends online? Or solo?
- If the son was playing with friends, could that be a protective factor?
- What is the potential result of the father taking away that social network?
- What other motivation would the son have for playing Xbox? Is it simply entertainment or something more?
- What if the son had a mental illness or disability? Would that affect his game play?
- Is the father a risk factor or a protective factor in this situation?

PREVENTION SCIENCE

The question of how to prevent behaviors is behind prevention science. Prevention science is an interdisciplinary application of scientific methodology that works to prevent or lessen negative human behavior and dysfunctions. It's a model used in fields such as behavioral health, substance abuse treatment and research, addiction, public health, and more. In addition, prevention science informs social and public policy.

The model of prevention science is particularly used in public health. Reviews of public health prevention programs found a higher rate of return than other interventions. In public health programs the focus is on preventing chronic diseases like diabetes, mental illness, and autoimmune illnesses. Other public health programs aim at improving environmental conditions that will affect a community's health. This could be adding sidewalks, improving a public park, making sure there is clean drinking water, and reducing lead in homes.

Despite a proven rate of return and findings that prevention programs improve the quality of life, there is far more government investment in intervention rather than prevention. It's understandable that intervention is where the money goes. Intervention treatments are more easily quantified, and there's direct contact with the community or individual. However, more money can be saved through education than incarceration, and by making environmental changes rather than cleaning up.

Did You Know?
One of the most researched and well-known examples of a prevention-based program is the nurse-family partnerships. This national model has specially trained nurses visit young, first-time pregnant moms, who have more risk factors than your average soon-to-be mother. The nurses visit the moms early in the pregnancy through the child's second birthday. They become a trusted resource, providing education and emotional support for a healthy pregnancy and child. It's estimated that for every dollar spent with nurse-family partnerships, almost six dollars in future costs for high risk families are saved.

Prevention science seeks to mitigate damaging human behaviors before they start. In contrast, intervention treats the behaviors once they are there. This is typically the approach in schools. Something happens, whether it be a rash of teen suicides, a school shooting, or an increase of cyberbullying incidents, and then programs are designed to confront the problems. It's a reactive rather than proactive mind-set. And while intervention programs are important and certainly help, they do little to decrease or eliminate the underlying issues that created the situation in the first place.

Intervention is preferable with parents, policy makers, and educators. Emotions are high, and you feel like you're *doing* something. Beating an Xbox with a baseball bat *feels* satisfying, cathartic even. Holding a school assembly about not doing drugs with a celebrity *feels* good. Taking away a device and putting it in a box during class *feels* like the problem is gone.

While prevention science is a research-backed approach, it's not very satisfying. It's not flashy; it can't be condensed into a simple slogan. A principal can feel an immediate effect by having an assembly, while with a prevention program, the changes of behavior take years to develop. This can cause frustration. And when other community members, staff, and parents are demanding a solution from those in charge, the flashier intervention approach that can be implemented quickly and doesn't have to be maintained for years is very appealing.

If schools and organizations want to combat the very real problems around technology, using the prevention model rather than intervention is the best chance for long-lasting individual and cultural changes. These changes will take time, support, research, and work, but fortunately, the blueprint already exists through decades of work by researchers, practitioners, and academics in the field of prevention science.

RISK AND PROTECTIVE FACTORS

A risk factor is a potential cause of dysfunctional human behavior. Typically, there are multiple risk factors that affect behavior. The field of suicide prevention has compiled a list of risk factors for adolescents who are more likely to commit suicide. The Centers for Disease Control (CDC) lists these factors, which include using alcohol and other drugs, being a victim of childhood abuse, and being male. Having one or even all these risk factors does not mean a teen will commit suicide, but it's a predictor. Knowing that an individual has several risk factors for suicide is a warning. The risk factors can alert parents and educators to intervene and pay closer attention to that person. It can also help administrators and policy makers make the best program decisions.

In contrast to a risk factor, a protective factor is something that can inhibit or stop the dysfunction from occurring. Like risk factors, a multitude of protective factors affect behavior, and just because an individual has several protective factors does not mean the problem behavior won't occur. In suicide prevention, the CDC lists protective factors that include family and community connectedness, access to mental health care, and skills in problem solving and conflict resolution. Knowing the protective factors for behaviors can also help policy makers. By supporting prevention and intervention programs that encourage protective factors, leaders can know that they are giving their community the best shot at stopping problems.

People do not develop their behaviors in a vacuum; they are highly influenced by the systems, structures, and people around them. Therefore, the prevention science model works on the individual, family/relationship, and the larger community. There are unique risks and protective factors for the individual; that individual's close relationships; and where that person works, goes to school, and/or lives.

Using the suicide prevention example, here are the combinations of factors that increase the risk.

- Individual: Impulsive or aggressive tendencies
- Relationship: Family history of suicide
- Community: Local epidemics of suicide

Implementing the prevention science model is a holistic approach and forces decision-makers to look beyond their own area.

Unlike prevention science, the field of digital citizenship is in its infancy. Much more research is needed. But behind any screen is a person. And while technology changes rapidly, human behavior does not. By focusing on our understanding of brain development, human behavior, and prevention science, we can determine risk and protective factors in digital citizenship.

One example of a risk factor in digital citizenship is cyberbullying. According to the United States government resource on bullying, StopBullying.gov, someone who is cyberbullied is more likely to bully someone else; therefore, being cyberbullied is a risk factor for cyberbullying. Using the cyberbullying example, having a supportive peer group would be a protective factor for not being a cyberbully.

Behavior	Risk Factors	Protective Factors
Victim of cyberbullying	LGBTQ, has a disability, female, middle school aged	Positive peer group, school-wide bullying policies
Perpetrator of cyberbullying	Victim of cyberbullying, middle school aged, female, more popular in school, mental health concerns	Kindness/civility programs, Family support and connectedness, school-wide bullying policies
Being hacked, personal information stolen	Lack of understanding of online privacy	Knowledge of online privacy issues
Sexting with strangers	Lack of connection	Family and community support
Excessive screen time	Boredom, Lack of connection	Family and community support, afterschool programs

Figure 2.1. Risk and protective factors related to digital citizenship. *Courtesy of the author*

Through the author's work with hundreds of students of different ages and backgrounds, plus previous prevention science research, she has picked out some risk and protective factors for unhealthy digital behavior.

Certain populations may have more risk factors than others. These include individuals with physical or mental disabilities, LGBTQ+ young people, and youth in foster care. It's understandable that foster care parents may be more protective than normal. There are strong feelings from both parents and practitioners. Research from the First Star Academy finds that individuals in foster care are less likely to graduate high school, have a higher risk of psychiatric disorders, and are more likely to attempt suicide.

Thus, programs like First Star Academy, digital citizenship classes, and other prevention programs are especially important. When schools are aware of risk factors, they can make a bigger impact. Investing and focusing on groups, schools, or individuals with multiple risk factors is a better use of valuable staff time and funds.

DIGITAL VIOLENCE AND TRAUMA

Caitlin White described her story of trauma in a first-person blog on *Medium*, "Digital Trauma."

> In my physical life, I was having dinner with my siblings, who don't use Twitter or share themselves online publicly very often . . . but my online self, an important part of my identity—and as a journalist, my professional career—was suddenly embroiled in scathing criticism and mocking ridicule. I was frozen, stung; the poison pooled and spread into my evening. Physical chills coursed through my body, my appetite disappeared. It was excruciating.

The CDC has well-documented lists of risk and protective factors for a range of dysfunctional behavior: suicide, child abuse, neglect, and more. One that relates to digital citizenship is violence. Bullying is violence, whether it be virtual or in-person. Individuals can be sexually assaulted online, as well as in person. While the medium may vary, the effects of violence remain the same.

Recognizing that digital violence was on the rise, the CDC put out a report in 2008 about "electronic aggression." In the report, it said: "As technology becomes more affordable and sophisticated, rates of electronic aggression are likely to continue to increase, especially if appropriate prevention and intervention policies and practices are not put into place." Research on violence connects violence and trauma. Trauma is an emotional response to a terrible event. After a traumatic event happens, individuals can experience shock and denial, and reactions may linger for years, including PTSD, flashbacks, or even physical symptoms like nausea or headaches. Trauma continues to reoffend, and the results of violence, even digital violence, can stay with an individual and be a risk factor for other types of dysfunctional behavior. Trauma-informed care is part of prevention science; it treats the whole individual.

In their Electronic Aggression report the CDC also said: "Young people who are victims of internet harassment are significantly more likely than those who have not been victimized to use alcohol and other drugs, receive school detention or suspension, skip school, or experience in-person victimization." Extreme digital violence can be particularly harmful because there is a permanent record of the violence and witnesses to the violence can be affected. StopBullying.gov reports that witnesses to bullying can be even more upset than the victim. These witnesses are also at a higher risk of mental health issues related to their feelings of helplessness to the situation.

This digital trauma can particularly hurt young people, who are developing their identities. The internet is a wonderful tool for adolescents to explore, research, and find out who they are. In many ways, it's a safe environment to try on those identities; but it leaves a record. A temporary identity may turn into a long-lasting one through the video recorder of the internet.

Too often in the media, schools, and at home, digital behavior is dismissed. People may see fighting on Snapchat or Minecraft as trivial. "Roasting," "calling out," or "slamming" someone online can even be a badge of honor and something to inspire. Young adults, who particularly want to appear a certain way in front of their peers, are especially susceptible. Politicians, celebrities, and even businesses have found that they can receive a lot of attention through engaging in suspect digital communication. Wendy's, a national fast-food chain, has exponentially boosted their followers through "roasting" others online.

Electronic aggression is also overlooked because it doesn't leave a mark. However, research supported by the Substance Abuse and Mental Health Services Administration (SAMHSA) shows that the violence does not have to be physical to cause changes in the brain. When confronting dysfunctional digital behavior, those that work with youth should take threats and evidence of violence seriously. They should also recognize that the witnesses to online harassment, exposure to toxic digital content, and cyberbullying may be suffering as well.

PREVENTION SCIENCE SOLUTIONS

The evidence is mounting that digital violence is a growing issue with long-term effects. But what can be done? There is not just one solution in the prevention science model. It calls for tailored approaches that focus on risk factors not only in the individuals but in the community and family. Based on the author's work and research, following are some recommended solutions.

Motivational Interviewing (MI)

Motivational interviewing is a therapeutic technique used to elicit change from the client. It's commonly used in addiction and mental health work. In work with adolescents, this prevention-based approach has found success in preventing teen pregnancy and HIV.

Instead of a top-down approach from a counselor to client, teacher to student, or parent to child, MI encourages a partnership or companionship. The style is generally quiet, eliciting information from the person being interviewed to influence change. Open-ended questions are given to encourage self-efficacy and autonomy. All the conversation is done in a nonjudgmental, empathetic way with the mentor/counselor in a facilitator role.

Motivational interviewing used with digital citizenship might include such questions as:

- What type of person do you want to be online?
- How did you feel when you saw that online?
- How do you think your friend felt when she was cyberbullied?
- How do you want others to view you online?
- What kind of online record do you want to leave for others to see?

Try it out: Motivational interviewing comes easier through practice. Try role-playing this exchange between a teacher and high school student. What would you add or do differently?

Teacher: I know it can be hard to pay attention in class. *(Validate the student's experience.)*

Student: Yeah, it's boring.

Teacher: I understand that sometimes class can feel boring. But your laptop is distracting the other students. *(Share a direct statement on your stand of the situation.)*

Student: But laptops are allowed. You can't take mine away.

Teacher: You are right. But you use it a lot, even during class discussions. And the noise from your laptop can make it harder to hear others. *(Repeat direct statement on your stand of the situation.)*

Student: Well that's their problem, not mine.

Teacher: I hear you saying that you do not want to put away the laptop in class. *(Validate the student's feelings of not being ready for change.)*

Student: . . .

Teacher: It's up to you how you want to use your laptop in class. But consider the feelings of your classmates who are trying to learn. I know you have friends in class and want the best for them. *(Reframe the situation and make it clear that change is up to the student.)*

Parent Education

Parent trainings are a valuable part of encouraging relationship and community protective factors. They have been found to decrease delinquent behavior such as drug use, violence, unplanned pregnancies, vehicular collisions, and addressing mental health concerns.

The parent trainings can be provided through many different resources, such as: schools, Parent Teacher Associations (PTAs), clinics, libraries, recreational centers, police stations, and afterschool programs.

A good parent education program

- has free training
- is offered at times parents can attend
- has positive reinforcement as its model

In the author's experience, the most well-attended parent trainings included extrinsic incentives. For example, one middle school provided a free dinner for all parents who attended and talked to all the providers in the community. This middle school also had a community center where parents could get free diapers, coats, socks, books, and other resources.

When teaching digital citizenship to parents it is helpful to provide a handout with a list of resources and a place for them to take notes. If the group is small enough, set the seats in a circle to encourage sharing and discussion.

Some evidenced-based parent training programs are:

- Parents as Teachers: This home visiting model, like the nurse-family partnership model, has practitioners go into homes of parents with young children and educate them on developmental stages, play, and more.
- Positive Parenting Program (Triple P): This program encourages confidence in parents to manage their child's behavior. For children with more severe behavioral problems, there is a twelve-session parent-and-child-focused treatment.
- Defiant Teens: This program, outlined in a manual called "Your Defiant Teen" includes classes for teens to become more of a positive and active participant in the family.

Positive Behavioral Intervention and Supports (PBIS)

Positive Behavioral Intervention and Supports (PBIS) is a school-wide structure for addressing positive behaviors in staff and students. It uses a multi-tiered model that addresses all levels of the school: students, parents, and administrators. This type of model, generally referred to as a Multi-Tiered System of Supports (MTSS) is an umbrella term that includes positive behavioral interventions but can also address academic concerns, since behavior and grades are related. Initially developed through the 1997 reauthorization of the Individuals with Disabilities Education Act (IDEA), MTSS was intended for students with behavioral disorders, but has been broadened.

PBIS and the MTSS model support prevention science in that they look beyond the individual to the system around that person. PBIS involves establishing school policies, teaching social responsibility skills, educating on communication and cyberbullying, and involving and following up with faculty on the progress. Research has found PBIS reducing bullying behaviors and improving school climate. One study in 2011 found that a schoolwide PBIS program resulted in a 41 percent decrease in the number of office discipline referrals for bullying behaviors, and a 65 percent decrease in school suspensions.

This structure can be difficult to implement; it takes time and buy-in from all levels of staff. But the research supports this type of model for the systemic, long-term behavioral changes.

Social and Emotional Learning

A social-emotional learning (SEL) approach, also called "whole-child education," works to build social competence and resiliency, reduce delinquent behavior, and improve academic outcomes. SEL has had increased interest in recent years because of a meta-analysis published in *Child Development* in 2011 that found gains in academic achievement for students in SEL programs versus those not enrolled. Other research has supported this approach.

SEL works to create more engaged citizens, and this can go into the digital realm as well. Joan Duffell, the director of the Committee for Children, a global nonprofit promoting SEL, said, "SEL is not only fundamental to education, but it's fundamental to raising citizens who actually participate in democratic life."

Topics covered in SEL programs include:

- Recognizing and responding to bullying
- Time management
- Mindfulness
- Encouraging empathy
- Developing relationship skills
- Developing better communication and problem-solving skills

By focusing on those skills, students can not only navigate the physical world better, but can also be safer and healthier in a digital environment.

SEL is a prevention science approach, focused on risk factors. Some school districts, such as in Cleveland, have implemented rigorous PBIS school-wide SEL models after seeing outcomes. CASEL, a nonprofit assisting and evaluating SEL programs, has free resources on their website: https://casel.org/guide/.

EXAMPLE OF A DIGITAL CITIZENSHIP ACTIVITY USING PREVENTION SCIENCE

How can educators utilize the prevention science model in their practice? The first step is identifying risk factors. Some risk factors are listed in this chapter and others can be found on the CDC's website: https://www.cdc.gov/violenceprevention/index.html.

Remember, there is overlap in the risk and protective factors related to bullying and violence and suicide prevention. A 2016 study found crossover factors between bullying and teen dating violence, and more linkages between different types of delinquent behavior in adolescents continue to be found.

When looking over risk and protective factors in children and adolescents, common themes emerge. One theme is connectedness, feeling connected to family, peers, and the larger community. Another one is mental health, having resiliency, access to mental health care, and coping skills. By focusing on one or both of these two themes in prevention programs, there is a higher likelihood of success.

Entire digital citizenship lessons could be spent on sleep. At first glance, it doesn't seem to make much sense to focus on sleep patterns and behavior when teaching digital citizenship. But when you understand prevention science, it becomes clearer.

Lack of sleep is a risk factor for aggression, mental health issues, and impulsivity. And teens get far too little of it. The National Sleep Foundation reports that only 15 percent of teens get the amount of sleep their bodies need.

One reason for that lack of sleep is technology. Screens emit blue light, a specific range of the light spectrum, the same light that makes the sky blue. Blue light suppresses melatonin twice as much as other types of light. Therefore, staring at a screen before bed, as many young people do, impacts their quantity and quality of sleep.

In the activity, we share the science behind sleep, the effects of little sleep, and how technology impacts it. The students are asked to share on the board or on a worksheet when they most feel awake, and when they go to bed. After all the students write their sleep cycle on the board, we discuss how everyone has different sleep cycles and ask questions in the motivational interviewing style such as:

- When do you have to be at school in the morning?
- Is it hard to get up in the morning?
- Do you want to feel more rested at night?
- What is one way that you can get better sleep?
- Do you think you would wake up easier if you had your phone out in the morning instead of at night?

After the discussion, the students are given a worksheet that has "Good, Better, and Best" strategies for waking and going to bed. The teens discuss in groups or pairs what their personal strategy will be. In one class, a group of three girls decided they would text each other when they woke up about what they wanted to wear the next day, not late at night before. At no point in the lesson are the teens told what to do. While peers and communities are big influences, behavioral change comes from within.

See appendix E for a Sleep Plan Worksheet

STORY OF THE D.A.R.E. PROGRAM

If programs aimed at changing human behavior do not address risk factors, they will not be effective. One well-known example is the D.A.R.E. (Drug Abuse Resistance Education) program. In the 1980s, D.A.R.E. became the model many school districts nationwide used for drug and gang prevention education. Trained police officers delivered the curriculum, which essentially focused on teaching kids to "say no to drugs."

A meta-analysis of the program found that not only did it have little effect, it may have had a negative impact. The D.A.R.E. program included education about the different types of substances available, and their harmful effects. Some studies have found that the information about different substances led students to believe that tobacco wasn't that bad when compared to such drugs as heroin.

Prevention science has developed a list of risk factors for teen substance abuse. This list includes posttraumatic stress disorder, witnessing violence, and being a victim of sexual assault. The D.A.R.E. program did not address those risk factors.

People want to believe if we tell kids to "just say no," then they won't use drugs. People want to believe that video games cause school shootings. People grasp onto potential explanations—video games, mental illness, vaccines—because those explanations provide a clearer path to a solution.

However, wanting to believe something does not make it true. Human behavior can't always be explained, and there is not a clear path from risk factor to delinquent behavior. Protective factors come from the individual, that person's relationships, and the larger community. There's not one change that can fix the issue; it takes a deep-rooted coordinated approach.

So what can an educator do? A teacher cannot change the student's home life, but she can be aware of those issues. A teacher cannot cure a student's mental illness, but he can recommend that student to a school counselor. A teacher cannot solve intergenerational poverty, but she can understand the effects of poverty on digital access and adjust homework accordingly. It takes an individual, school, family, friends, and the entire community to increase those protective factors.

Are we addressing risk factors when we talk about digital citizenship? Are we really assessing the "whys" and digging deep into the causes? Are we simply banning or even smashing the device? Digital citizenship, like prevention science, is a discipline that is growing, and more research is needed. But perhaps the first step is looking beyond the screen.

3

Assessing Digital Citizenship Knowledge

WHAT DO YOU KNOW? KNOWLEDGE ASSESSMENT

What do you know about digital citizenship? Was your first encounter with the term when you picked up this book? Or has your organization been implementing digital citizenship principles for years? And if they are, what are they covering and how effective is that work? When you hear the words *digital citizenship* what comes to mind?

This chapter will help you find the gaps in your own knowledge of digital citizenship, as well as gaps in information in your organization and with your students.

GAP ANALYSIS

A gap analysis compares the reality of knowledge and performance with the potential. It's typically conducted in a business environment, but the principles can be used in any field. Gap analyses help organizations know where to start. They create a foundation to build upon. If there is no foundation to a house, you cannot build on top of it.

A gap analysis helps answer these questions:

- Where are you?
- Where do you want to go?
- What will you do to get there?
- How important is getting there?
- Who is responsible for leading the way?

A sample gap analysis can be found in appendix A and can be used for evaluating both individual and organizational gaps. The sample gap analysis divides the nine standards of digital citizenship into three categories: Respect, Educate, and Protect. Mike Ribble, who elucidated the nine standards of digital citizenship, divided it into those three categories to help with curriculum development. By grouping the elements of digital citizenship into categories on the gap analysis, individuals can more easily evaluate performance and knowledge.

The sample gap analysis is set up to make action happen. Perhaps that action is more education of the individual or organization's staff. Perhaps that action is implementing existing institutional knowledge. Whatever the case may be, the goal of the analysis is not only to determine what you know, but how to get there.

On the sample gap analysis, there are two important boxes to fill out. One is "Priority" and the other is "Ownership." Progress can be stalled without clearly defining those two areas.

You can determine the priority of the action by many different means. Rank the actions from 1 to 3, with 1 being the highest priority. Clarify the priority by grouping higher priority items with shorter time periods. For example, a high-priority item must be completed in the next month. Medium priority the next quarter. Low priority the next calendar year. Whatever method is used to define priority, what's important is that those reading and sharing the gap analysis have a common understanding.

Ownership defines who is responsible for leading the action. It does not mean that a person is *doing* the action; the person might just be supervising or coordinating it. This can be an individual, a division, or a small group. Whoever it is, the responsible person or group must make sure the action happens and then evaluate the performance of that action. This can mean following up with team members working on the issue, and comparing the current state to the desired state.

After completing a gap analysis, put it in a prominently visible spot. Tack it on a bulletin board. Make copies and distribute them. Tape it on a mirror. The worksheet can be a continual reminder of the goals created.

This sample gap analysis can be adapted to other digital citizenship goals. Perhaps your organization wants to focus on one specific area of digital citizenship. The main categories at the top would stay the same; it would just be the categories that would differ.

EXAMINING ORGANIZATIONAL KNOWLEDGE

Digital citizenship is a multidisciplinary subject that may encompass many different roles in an organization. When Digital Respons-Ability, an organization devoted to digital citizenship, connected our student workshop learning outcomes to Common Core standards, we found connections in several subjects:

- mathematics
- career and technical education
- libraries and/or media centers
- English
- computer science
- health science

Therefore, to examine a school's knowledge of digital citizenship means including multiple staff in different subject areas. And to make that coordinated change requires a community impact model.

Examining organizational knowledge and creating an action plan can be difficult because of the wide array of ownership. Does the library media specialist take the lead? The computer science teacher? While both of those roles should be involved, a coordinated approach would include organizational leadership that has authority and purview over multiple areas of ownership. If an organization's digital citizenship plan is implemented just under one specific group, then there will be missing pieces. A gap analysis can help organizations put all those pieces together and decide on ownership so the work moves forward instead of being siloed in one area.

EXAMINING STUDENT KNOWLEDGE

A frequent question Digital Respons-Ability has received when administering evaluation tools to students is: What is digital citizenship? It's not necessarily a widely used term, particularly to a seventh grader. The first thing to do when examining student knowledge is to explain what the term means, and what it encompasses.

Some ways to describe digital citizenship to younger people who have not heard the term include:

- **Make the connection between a real-life citizen and a digital one:** "A good citizen is someone who's involved in the community, who follows the laws, and cares about what happens in the world. Being a good digital citizen is the same except the community is online."
- **Talk about digital citizenship in terms of the individual:** "Who do you want to be? Who do you want to be online? Are your actions online supporting who you want to be?"

KNOWLEDGE, ATTITUDES, AND BEHAVIOR

As was said in chapter 2, the study of digital citizenship should focus on the person behind the screen. The cell phone is not being surveyed, the individual is. To test the understanding and impact of digital citizenship, three domains of the individual should be surveyed: knowledge, attitudes, and behavior.

A report in the *Performance Improvement* journal summarizes some of the research of how knowledge, attitudes, and behavior (also known as the KAB approach) influences changes in behavior. It is also sometimes referred to as KAP with the *P* standing for *practice*. The report states, "Behaviors can inform attitudes . . . attitudes are influential in attention. Thus, attitudes can impact what an individual perceives, and therefore impacts knowledge gains." All three domains—knowledge, attitudes, and behavior—work together to make change. If only one is focused on, or evaluated, the whole individual is not being studied.

To be a full digital citizen, a person must have some knowledge of digital principles and digital law and be able to navigate and use the internet. They must have an attitude of critical thinking, skepticism of bias, and recognition of how their actions online can be permanent. And fully participating digital citizens also must have behaviors that contribute to their own emotional and physical well-being, and actions that make them creators, not just consumers.

Certain digital citizenship elements are evaluated through the KAB approach. The table below summarizes which elements are most easily examined through the different domains.

Table 3.1. Knowledge, Attitudes, and Behavior in Digital Citizenship

Knowledge	Digital Commerce	Digital Rights and Responsibilities	Digital Literacy
Attitudes	Digital Communication	Digital Etiquette	Attitudes toward the subject of digital citizenship
Behaviors	Digital Health and Wellness	Digital Safety and Security	Behaviors toward the subject of digital citizenship

When evaluating individuals, question them on all three domains. Conduct a pre- and posttest survey to examine their knowledge, attitudes, and behaviors before any digital citizenship programs and after.

Sample questions to examine student knowledge, attitude, and behavior include:

- Do you know what digital citizenship is?
- What do you think about when you hear the words *digital citizenship*?
  - Follow-up questions can include, "What do you think about when you hear the words *digital access*?" The same can be asked for other elements of digital citizenship.
- How do you feel about digital citizenship? Do you want to learn more about it?
  - Follow-up questions can include, "What do you feel about online privacy now?" and other elements of digital citizenship.

- Have you changed anything about what you do online?
  - Follow-up questions can include specific questions related to screen time, communication, online purchases, and so on.
- What element of digital citizenship do you know the most about?
- What makes you anxious online? What makes you happy online?

Surveys are just one method for determining behavioral change. They are a simple method that can cover all three domains. All testing tools come with issues. Self-reporting can be problematic and improper questions can guide subjects to incorrectly report. There is no perfect method to evaluate, but by using tools that cover all three domains and multiple ways to test, more conclusive evidence can be found.

Some other testing tools and examples of how to use those tools include:

Knowledge

- **Forced choice testing:** Create a multiple-choice survey that tests vocabulary and knowledge of digital citizenship.
- **Concept mapping:** Have students create a concept map that connects the elements of digital citizenship in different relationships.

Attitudes

- **Test on a continuum:** Use testing tools like a Likert scale to examine how students feel about certain digital citizenship subjects.

Behaviors

- **Interviews:** Interview students before and after programs on any changes they have made outside of the organization. Family and peers of the individual can also be interviewed to track any behavioral changes.
- **Measuring outcomes:** Use different software to track screen time.

SETTING GOALS

After the training or program is completed, what happens next? How do you retain knowledge? Will attitudes shift after the program? How do you make long-term changes in behaviors? One method is creating goals.

A gap analysis is helpful for institutional goals, but not ideal for personal goals. If an organization wants to implement change, it must view the system and individual working in coordination with each other. Individuals make ground-up changes to organizations. Organizations trickle down change to individuals. Both are needed.

When personal goals fail, it's because of several reasons. The goal may be too big and unattainable. People may give up because they just don't know where to start.

The goal may have no timeline. For example, if someone makes a goal to lose weight but does not set a date of when they will reach that goal, it's easy to procrastinate. Personal goals may also fail because the individual does not have the resources to accomplish the goal. For example, if someone wants to learn to ice skate, but doesn't have an ice rink nearby. When people don't reach their goals, it can create discouragement and demotivate them. Organizations don't want demotivated staff, so they must help create guidelines and timelines for their staff's goals.

One popular method for goal setting is SMART Goals. The acronym SMART standards for Specific, Measurable, Attainable, Relevant, Timely. An example of a digital citizenship SMART goal for a teacher would be: *Incorporate a media-literacy activity once a week through fall semester.*

- **S (Specific):** Adding media-literacy education to class
- **M (Measurable):** Tracking each week throughout the semester to make sure the media-literacy activity occurred.
- **A (Attainable):** This is something that the teacher has time to implement and the knowledge to implement.
- **R (Relevant):** Media literacy is something this teacher has identified as a digital citizenship issue in the classroom.
- **T (Timely):** This goal will be reached by doing one activity a week for the fall semester.

When creating a SMART goal, it's suggested to make sub-goals, breaking the goal down into smaller, specific parts. An example of sub-goals for adding media literacy activities in a classroom can include:

- Compiling a list of media-literacy activities
- Specifying the time and the day of the week the activities will occur
- Researching media-literacy issues
- Notifying the students that these activities will occur

Setting goals cannot guarantee success. Change can be slow and patterns hard to break. But it can provide a clear path from point A to B.

It's hard to know how to get somewhere, if you don't know where you are. Evaluating individual and organizational knowledge gives you your location, which helps set the destination. Sometimes organizations are reactive. There's a parent complaint, a teen suicide, bad press, or any number of negative incidences that can put institutions in crisis mode. While in that mode, it's tempting to rush on ahead; but driving fast can also make the destination farther away. Assessing knowledge is a preventative measure that provides a clear path forward.

4

Teaching Models for Digital Citizenship

Digital citizenship is a new discipline that covers multiple subjects. So how is it best taught? This chapter explores three research-based models of teaching—gamification, experiential learning, and student-led learning—that the author has used in the field.

GAMIFICATION

> *Trying to teach a large group of elementary students is tough. Teaching them after lunch is harder. I was leading a discussion on positive things to do online and wasn't getting the engagement I wanted. I was working hard to steer the conversation in a positive way, but as often happens when talking about things online, it was going in the opposite direction.*
>
> *Then I had an idea—I wouldn't have the students talk about the positive things, I would have them draw it. And I would turn that drawing into a game of Pictionary. Students would draw what makes them happy online and the other students would have to guess. There were no prizes, no scoreboard, but the students started sitting up and getting excited. Soon voices were piping up guessing the drawing and by the end we had a long list of positive things to do online.*
>
> —*Story from the author*

Toddlers to seniors love games. We are born loving games. An infant who cannot walk or talk will enjoy a game of peekaboo. Throughout human history, games have been found across all cultures. Clark Aldrich, author and game designer said, "Games are a more natural way to learn than traditional classrooms. . . . Not only have humans been playing games since the beginning of our species, but intelligent animals as well." Why is it, then, that games are sometimes seen as trivial or not educational? And why do we not have more games in a classroom?

Games in classrooms are nothing new, but technology has added more opportunities and variety for games. However, technology is not *required* to gamify a lesson. *Gamification* refers to adding elements of gaming in a non-game context. Some of those elements may be dividing groups into teams, awarding a prize, showcasing winners on a board, adding "levels" to learning or increasingly hard challenges, or creating characters and narratives.

Tech companies are well versed about gamification in getting engagement. For example, Snapchat has Snapstreaks. It's a challenge to see how long you can keep snapping an individual. If you've snapped enough within twenty-four hours, you get a prize, an emoji fire next to your name. And if you haven't snapped enough, a timer appears to let you know that your streak is ended. This gamification has paid off, with teens spending more hours trying to up their streaks.

Tech companies have also used gamification in more positive ways, like Google's Interland. This interactive adventure game, aimed at elementary school ages, teaches some digital citizenship principles to children such as being careful what you share online and being kind and respectful to others. Players steer a 3-D robot figure through challenges and games.

Like other subjects, gamification is a model that works with digital citizenship. Digital citizenship is about self-efficacy. Students need to choose who they want to be online. Gamification encourages autonomy by having the lesson not be a traditional top-down lesson, but one where the student takes an active role. Educators are more like facilitators in a gamified lesson rather than authority figures.

Gamification has its pros and cons. But even simple tweaks can change up a traditional lecture into an experience.

Table 4.1. Pros and Cons of Gamification

Pros	*Cons*
Creates positive feelings of enjoyment and engagement	Can encourage negative behaviors through competition
Can motivate some students	Can be detrimental to intrinsic motivation
Can encourage experiential learning	Lack of resources for incentives such as prizes, badges, and awards
Give students opportunity to have more autonomy in learning	May not motivate all students

EXPERIENTIAL LEARNING

The second grader stood in front of the classroom grinning. She was a living robot, being "programmed" with directions from her classmates. "Go left!" shouted one boy. "Wait," said another student, "she can't go left, she's not looking that way." The instructor nodded to the student's comment. "Now what does she have to do before she goes left?" Upon receiving the correct program, the girl turned and took a step left. She was one step closer to completing the robot maze and demonstrating basic computational thinking.

—Story from the author

Computational thinking could be taught in a variety of ways—lecture, video, a worksheet—but those means might not encourage a very important way humans learn: through doing. Experiential learning is doing something, then reflecting upon that action. The students in the living robot activity actively told the robot what to do, and then reflected on their methods. Instead of knowledge being transmitted from the top down, like from a teacher to a student, it bubbled up from the bottom. In experiential learning, the teacher is a guide or facilitator. They coax the students to the right answer instead of delivering it to them.

A vital part of experiential learning is reflection. Learners should contemplate what they did, why it happened one way, why it didn't happen another way, and to extrapolate that knowledge to other topics. In the living robot activity, a teacher can facilitate learning and self-reflection and introduce new concepts by such statements as these:

- *How should the robot move first? Why?*
- *Does anyone see any mistakes? Where the commands don't match up with what the robot is supposed to do? Those mistakes are called bugs.*
- *Does anyone else notice something about our algorithm? There is a pattern of steps right here, where the robot goes up, turns left, and then turns right again. That pattern is called a loop.*
- *Was there a better way for the robot to go through that maze? Let's try it again and see if we can do it in less steps.*
- *Do you think a computer could improve on the steps for our living robot? Computers can learn by doing too. We call that machine learning.*

The questions force the student to contemplate further on the activity and they introduce new concepts in a way that's more understandable. An instructor can provide the definition of an algorithm, but the student is more likely to remember that definition when it's reinforced through doing and a real-life example.

The living robot activity taught one element of digital citizenship: digital literacy. Students were introduced to how computers think and new vocabulary. While this lesson was aimed at elementary students, it can be scaled for secondary ages. For example, older students might have the technical know-how to code a set of commands on a computer to complete a certain task. Free online software like Scratch could be used. A teacher could divide the class into teams, create a specific goal, and let the students experiment with different commands. This also uses the gamification model by having teams compete on who can get to the goal the fastest.

See appendix B for a sample lesson plan of the living robot activity.

What Is Experiential Learning?

Humans naturally learn by trying to figure things out. Think of infants. When we are very young, we learn what things are by touching, shaking, throwing, and putting things in our mouths. Infants cannot verbalize questions, nor do they have the vocabulary or knowledge to understand the verbal instructions coming from adults. They must learn through their senses: touch, taste, smell, hearing—by experimenting. Infants learn that an object falls by throwing it, what an object is made of by tasting it, and what an object sounds like by shaking it.

Despite this being the organic process by which all people learn, many traditional classroom settings take a very different approach. Students receive knowledge, not create it. Students are shown pictures, text, or video of an object, they do not touch, taste, or smell it. Students are encouraged to accept the answers of others, not generate those answers themselves.

This is not to say that classrooms cannot educate students, certainly not. Classrooms are a scalable model that can educate a larger group of people on specific tasks in a certain amount of time. They produce educated students all the time. There are reasons most societies use the traditional model. Experiential learning is harder to scale, coordinate, and evaluate. Our physical, indoor structures don't always lend themselves to experimentation. And importantly, it is easier to test knowledge through an exam rather than an activity. While experiential learning may never be normalized in traditional classrooms throughout the world, it still is a valuable tool for education and teaching digital citizenship.

Steps of Experiential Learning

David Kolb is an educational theorist who, with Ron Fry, developed the experiential learning model in the 1970s. This model has always existed in learning. Aristotle wrote about the concepts in his *Nicomachean Ethics*. In addition, Kolb built upon the work of John Dewey, who said, "We do not learn from experience . . . we learn from reflecting on experience." From those past experts and existing concepts Kolb articulated a clear visual model and advocated for the process in recent years.

The steps of experiential learning are:

1. Concrete experience
2. Reflective observation
3. Abstract conceptualization
4. Active experimentation

The cycle starts with a concrete experience that leads to another experience through experimentation, which repeats the cycle. In the living robot example, the concrete experience was the activity directing the student through the maze. Through that activity, and after it, the teacher-facilitator asks questions that prompt reflection and

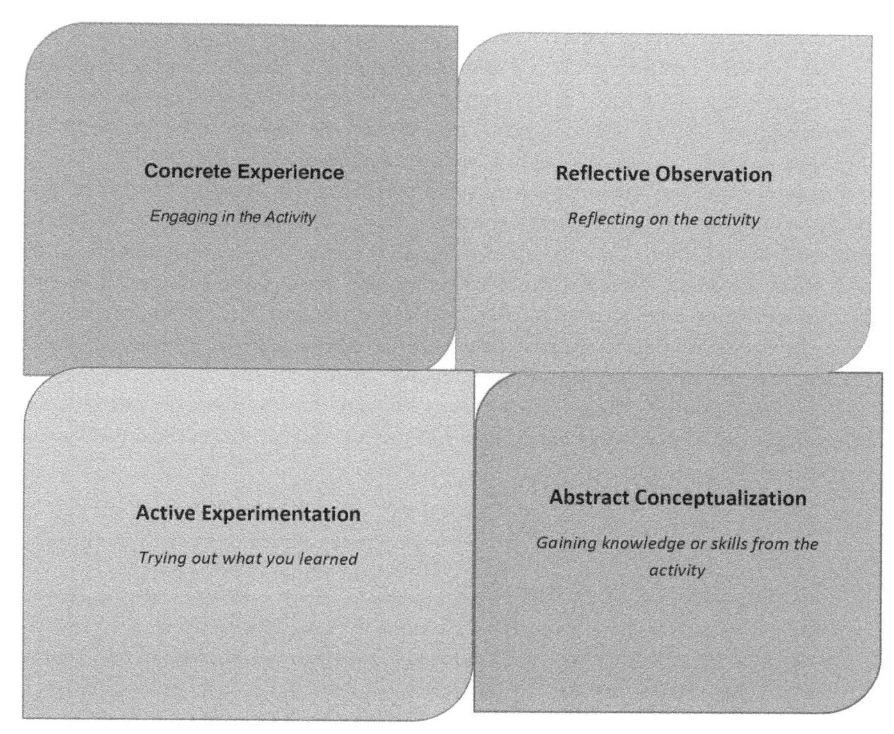

Figure 4.1. Kolb's Experiential Learning Model. ***Courtesy of the author***

conceptualization of other concepts, like machine learning. Then another student is assigned to be the living robot, but this time students are encouraged to experiment to decrease the number of commands used to get the robot through the maze.

Kolb said that for genuine knowledge to be learned from this experiential learning process, the student must have existing abilities. The students must be actively engaged, be able to reflect on the activity, and possess analytical and problem-solving skills to use the knowledge gained from the experimentation.

An educator does not need to be an expert on experiential learning to use this theory in a classroom. There are simple questions that can be asked during reflective observation.

1. What did you notice?
2. Why do you think that happened?
3. Does that happen in real life?
4. Why do you think that happens?
5. How could you use this?

Other ways to encourage reflection are by utilizing journals. Throughout the lessons in class students can add to their journal, writing their thoughts about the experiences. A teacher can write a daily prompt on the board that students use to write a paragraph or two in their journal. The journals can also be used to sketch out thoughts or map concepts, instead of writing sentences.

Educators can also encourage parts of the experiential learning process in their assignments and traditional lectures. For example, a teacher can stop the lecture, pair students together, and have them think about what they learned and share that with their classmate. After that brief reflecting and sharing, the lecture can resume. Traditional lectures are often like a firehose, lots of information coming out quickly. It can be overwhelming to students. By pausing to reflect, share, journal, or sketch, the students can better absorb the information.

The experiential learning model is used beyond the classroom in business and other fields. No matter what the exact subject being taught, this cyclical process can deepen learning.

This chapter focuses primarily on the positives of experiential learning, but there are negatives. It's not a model that can be used effectively in every scenario. Experiential learning can be difficult to implement because of behavior issues. Large classrooms make it difficult to provide the level of guided reflection and discussion needed to reinforce the learning. Some students may need a firmer hand and step-by-step instructions in an activity, which is also harder with many students. Another negative of experiential learning is that it can take more time. A traditional lecture gets straight to the point, releasing the information directly. Experiential learning coaxes the information and learning out in an iterative process. When teachers are crunched for time, or must cover a very specific set of materials for an upcoming test, experiential learning may not be the best teaching model.

Experiential Learning and Digital Citizenship

Like gamification, experiential learning is a meaningful model for teaching digital citizenship. To be productive and smart digital citizens, students must be able to problem-solve, reflect on what they see online, and be able to absorb and disseminate knowledge. Students need to reflect on both their own and others' online behavior. They must know how to critically examine communication and content, which is being given to them like a firehose.

Digital citizenship encourages students to move from consumers to creators. We create when we feel knowledgeable and comfortable about a subject. You cannot just sit a student down at a computer and expect them to create a viable code. They must experiment first. They must understand the concepts of coding before they can apply them.

Experiential learning gives students both the knowledge and the confidence to create new things. Students need that confidence. They need to be confident enough to fail. Experimentation is about failing and trying again and again. Think of the example of riding a bike. The first time you ride a bike, an adult is there to help. That adult might hold on to the bars while you push the pedals. You may fall a few times, but you'll be helped up again. In the beginning the adult stays by your side, encouraging you. But eventually you're by yourself and you must pedal and steer alone. Riding first with a trusted adult, where you know you won't fall, helps you feel more comfortable with trying by yourself.

Most of the time students are online they don't have a trusted adult near them. They don't have someone sitting by their side coaching and steering. Students must learn to ride by themselves. Experiential learning will help get them pedaling.

STUDENT-LED LEARNING

When a group of junior high students were surveyed on their favorite and least-favorite activities in a series of digital citizenship classes, some clear favorites emerged. One of those favorites was called "Game Plan" where the students developed their own bedtime and wake up plan around technology. This activity asks them to take the information around technology and sleep and decide what they wanted to do. There was no right or wrong, no test, just them conferring with each other to make decisions about their learning.

—Story from the author

In a typical day of a junior high student, how often are they directed to do things? When they wake up, they may be reminded not to forget their homework, given a breakfast, or forced to choose between two options. At school, they may have six teachers telling them what to do. The class bell directs them where they go next. After school, their homework makes the decision for much of their free time. They learn what their classes teach, which may not leave much time for any hobbies or pursuing their own curiosities. A junior high student's bedtime may not be chosen by them but the adult in their house. From when they wake up to when they decide to sleep, the directions they take and what they learn are mostly predetermined. Individuals who are growing and maturing and just a few years from being independent certainly have little control over their learning.

Providing opportunities for self-direction, for youth to take the lead, not only encourages learning, it also allows students some much-needed desire for control and autonomy in their lives. Student-led learning, also known as peer programs or youth-led programming, refers to students taking a larger role in the teaching, activity, or initiative.

It's a model used frequently in public health and programs such as substance abuse prevention, suicide prevention, and more. Students are highly influenced by their peers, hour-for-hour spending more time with them than with adults. A meta-analysis by the Advocates of Youth nonprofit reviewed twenty-eight published peer-led programs and found that over the last two decades that "peer programs can have statistically significant effects on attitudes, norms, knowledge, behaviors, and health and achievement outcomes."

While the approach has typically been in the health sector, youth-led programs have also been studied in bullying and peer-aggression, an area that digital citizenship addresses. A 2014 study in the *Journal of Early Adolescence* found that using the youth-led model in middle schools found "significant improvements" in the knowledge and attitudes of the students and "significant reductions" in anxiety, and recommended the approach for peer aggression in school settings.

Student-led learning is part of creating digital behavioral changes in schools and communities. However, it must be done right. Participation by the youth must be genuine. Adults must allow them decision-making authority and celebrate the student's success, rather than co-opt that success for their own gain. Hart's Ladder of Participation gives a visual framework to practitioners to find the best balance between student and adults in decision-making. There are different degrees, or rungs on the ladder, of participation.

- Manipulation: The lowest rung, where adults have total authority and use the students' voices and ideas for themselves.
- Decoration: One step above, which only involves students in a limited capacity such as students given a script.
- Tokenism: Youth only have a limited voice, such as being placed on a panel for the "youth voice" but not deciding what the panel is or given much time to speak.
- Young people are consulted and informed: Adults may start the project but the voices of students are given equal weight.
- Adult-initiated, shared decisions: Adults have the initial idea but young people are involved in planning, implementing, and making decisions on the project.
- Young people lead and initiate action: Young people initiate the project but consult available adults if needed.
- Young people and adults share decision-making: This is the top rung of the ladder where young people have the ideas, implement the projects, and invite adults to join them as equal partners.

Not all organizations and classrooms can allow for the highest rungs of the ladder. There are often policies that prevent such decision-making, particularly when it involves multiple partners or budgets. Student-led learning can also be hard to implement because often the decision-making powers are with administrators and officials that do not work directly with students. Students are far-removed from those projects and decisions.

For example, students may wish to change the school's technology policy, but they are not involved in the meetings by the technology staff, principals, and school administrators who develop the policy. The policy may also have been created years ago in reaction to an incident. In addition to being left out of conversation, students aren't necessarily educated on the policies and processes to change and implement policy. The desire to change it may be there, but not the know-how of what to do. Despite limitations, Hart's Ladder of Participation gives a framework and an ideal to work with youth to make positive changes.

Beyond behavioral change, involving students in decision-making creates a higher success rate of those decisions being effective. Nancy Watson said regarding student involvement, "I always use Jason Ohler's quote, 'students who help frame the system are a lot less likely to game the system.' Kids will have buy-in on rules that they help create. [It's] much more effective than to just 'lay down the law' or tell students all the things they shouldn't do." To use the technology policy example, if those rules were implemented without student input or consulting, then the students would be less likely to be aware of the rules, and follow them. Why should they? The policy means little to them beyond yet another thing throughout their waking hours they should do.

Student-Led Learning and Digital Citizenship

Adults can make all the policies and rules they want around, but ultimately, it's the youth who must make the decision of who they want to be online. By allowing youth space to take the lead, make decisions, and be part of the process, adults can teach the important "soft" skills needed to successfully navigate the online environment.

Following are some examples of student-led digital citizenship programs.

Student-led online challenges: Provide students online challenges to encourage the positives of technology. Some examples are in hashtags. The hashtag #usetech4good can be used by students to showcase positive examples. Another example that Watson provided is #digcitsnaps, which is using Snapchat to call out positive social media behavior. Students could also try the #digcit6wordstories challenge and talk about what digital citizenship means to them.

Student-led campaigns: Ask students what's important to them, and then help guide them for school- or community-wide campaigns on those subjects. Watson suggests, "get kids to come up with social media campaigns like anonymous 'atta-boys' for kindness or maybe a social justice cause that is important to them."

Allow students access: Instead of limiting official social media channels to a few professionals, allow the students access. For example, have the students make an online community group on subjects or events in the community and have administrators regularly consult and talk to the students about their thoughts on the group.

Students could also have posting privileges. One day a week, students can take over Twitter or Facebook to share items they find interesting or post about interesting or challenging things they're dealing with.

Showcase student achievement: Provide official online venues for students to share their work. For example, create a slider on a school website to show off some digital projects of students. Allow them space to shine while staying out of the way.

Invite them to adult spaces: Include youth at community meetings, and work hard to listen and support them to be there. This could be school community councils, PTA meetings, school board meetings, teacher trainings, or other official gatherings where such subjects as technology are discussed. It can be difficult for some youth to attend meetings because of transportation, so make a concentrated effort to provide that transportation or have meetings in a space and time where students can attend. Give them specific time on the agenda to share their thoughts, and try to call on them during a board meeting. This may be the first time this youth have been involved in an all-adult official meeting, so they may not understand the rules and processes. Mentor them and include them. To avoid tokenism, make a commitment that to the best of your ability their ideas will be implemented and seriously considered.

Provide them a budget: Put money behind your mouth; set aside funding to allow students' ideas to be implemented. Budgets are a barrier to peer programs because youth do not have access to funding or the decision-making power to change that funding. By deliberately setting aside funds for student-led projects each year, you encourage more participation. Money speaks and sends a message to students that "we trust you."

For example, if students decide that they want to work on a project that gives more digital access to students, allow them funds to purchase a device. Perhaps they will pick a device that's not the best for the environment; that's fine, failure is a learning tool. Throughout the process, they will learn budgeting skills, how to communicate in a group, how to research options, and about adult structures for implementing change.

It can be difficult to allow the space for student-led learning. Adults get scared: What if someone gets hurt? What if they post something potentially damaging? Those are legitimate fears, but consider the worst that can happen. Are lives in danger? Probably not. Are jobs in danger? No. Mistakes may be made, but those mistakes are great teachers. Adults also react in fear from deeper concerns. The younger generation can represent promise and optimism, but also represents our eventual decline into irrelevancy. We want to hold onto control, and allowing student-led learning is admitting "I don't know everything" and "eventually these students will be in charge, not me." That can be frightening. And technology is frightening enough. But wouldn't you rather have a new generation that is educated on digital citizenship and the effects of technology, rather than one that has not been guided or has been restricted their whole lives? Eventually they will be the ones making the policies and decisions, and it's the role of educators to make them as prepared as possible.

5

Technology Trends

Almost all of the many predictions now being made about 1996 hinge on the Internet's continuing exponential growth. But I predict the Internet will soon go spectacularly supernova and in 1996 catastrophically collapse.

—*Robert Metcalf (who is credited with having invented Ethernet)*

The future is notoriously hard to predict; bad predictions can be found throughout history from the beginning of humans' writing things down. Tech predictions are particularly difficult because of the rapid rate of change. This chapter will attempt tech predictions based on past and current trends and data. Trends in devices, demographics, screen time, gaming, ed tech, AI, and more will be explored as well as their implications for digital citizenship.

Educators who understand the trends can better prepare for the changes that will affect their students, classroom, and organization. Knowledge of technology changes and trends also informs the practice and teaching of digital citizenship. What may have worked when teaching some elements of digital citizenship a decade ago may not be as relevant now. Robert Metcalfe literally ate his regrettable words. He blended up a copy of his column with those quotes with liquid and drank it down.

One constant is change, and there will continue to be mistakes and unfortunate predictions made. But hopefully no future educators and practitioners of digital citizenship will feel the need to literally consume the evidence of their mistakes.

DIGITAL ACCESS

Digital access is a foundational element of digital citizenship. Without access, there is no opportunity to become a digital citizen. Access has changed dramatically over the last two decades. The computer labs in schools in the 1980s and 1990s were often the first and/or only access a student had to a computer and the internet. In the original Technology Foundation Standards for students by ISTE in 1998, there was more reference to the hard skills of learning how to use a computer. Digital citizenship was not a big part of the conversation. The concerns were getting devices to students, and teaching basic computer skills.

Now access has increased exponentially. The US Census Bureau has collected data periodically through their American Community Survey (ACS), tracking computer ownership. According to that data only 8 percent of American households owned a computer in 1984. That number rose rapidly in the 1990s. According to the United States Bureau of Labor Statistics, ownership rose from an average 15 percent in 1990 to 35 percent in 1997. It continued to rise in the 2000s with the ACS reporting 89 percent ownership in 2016.

That high of 89 percent ownership is because of smartphones, which are classified as computers according to census data. The actual number of computers at home stalled around 2010, while mobile device ownership rose. The numbers change when examining the specific devices. There is a growing number of individuals who are smartphone dependent, meaning they rely on smartphones to access the internet, not other devices. About one-fifth of Americans are smartphone dependent. This number is higher for non-whites and lower-income Americans. Only having a smartphone to access the internet can affect students' ability to research, create content, and complete their homework. While access is significantly higher than two decades ago, it's not equitable.

Another piece of data to examine more carefully is location. Access is not spread equally. The National Digital Inclusion Alliance evaluated the ACS data to break down what cities have availability of broadband access. About 30 percent of Americans do not have reliable broadband access, but that number balloons to over 60 percent in the worst-connected cities. In rural or lower-income areas, people are more likely to be smartphone dependent for their access or not have any access at home or in places near them.

Digital access has not improved equally for all populations. According to Pew Research, 95 percent of adults with a college or graduate degree use the internet. For those who have not graduated high school, that number drops to 66 percent. Household income also has strong effects on access. Households with higher incomes are more likely to be regular internet users, and have more devices at home. Race and ethnicity is another data point to evaluate. African Americans and Hispanics are less likely than whites or Asian Americans to use the internet. There are other divides in access for individuals with disabilities who may not be able to use devices because of impairments.

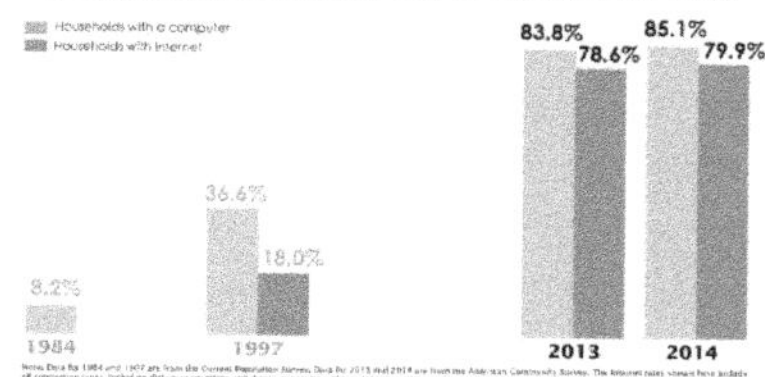

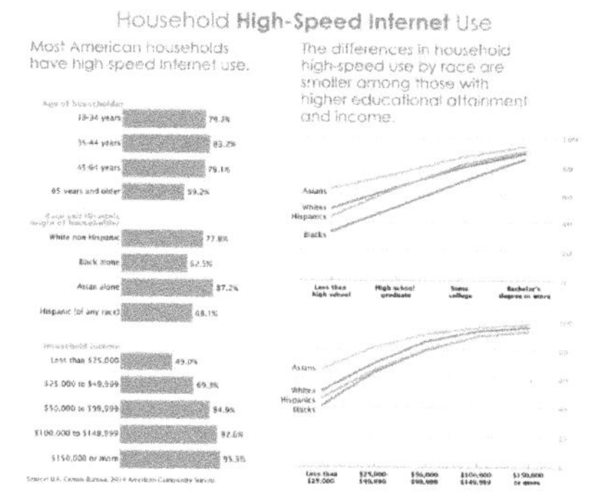

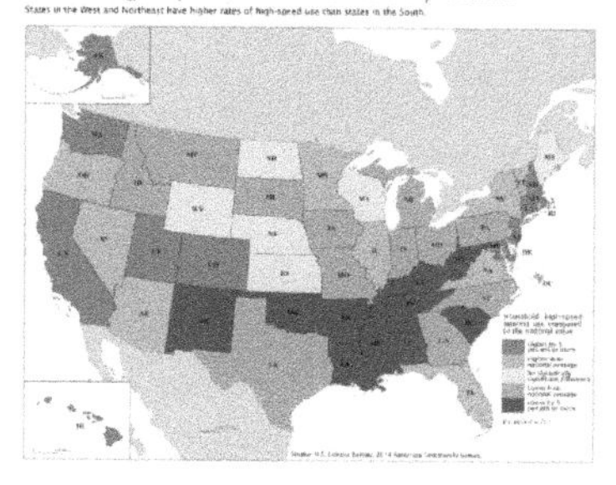

Figure 5.1. Household high-speed internet use. *U.S. Census Bureau*

Through Digital Respons-Ability's work we have worked extensively with students who are not digitally included. More about these populations will be shared in chapter 10. In fall of 2018 we taught a group of students in secure detention about digital citizenship. Since it is a secure facility, there are strong restrictions about bringing items in and what the students can access. The detention center had firm restrictions on technology. These students could not access the internet, and any time at a computer was highly supervised. While our program is set up to teach without technology, it still did hamper us. Written feedback from a supervisor at the detention advised that our program could be used with "actual use of technology demonstrations," which while helpful were not allowed.

Educators should keep in mind the population they are working with. Some students may not have reliable access at home. Other students may not have consistent access at school. And other students, like those in secure care, do not have access at all.

The gap in access is referred to as the "digital divide." The divide can affect long-term outcomes for students. And access is just one part of the divide. Digital inclusion encompasses more than just digital access.

Full digital inclusion means that an individual has:

1. a device that connects to the internet
2. digital literacy skills
3. affordable and reliable internet access

Students who are smartphone dependent may not be on the wrong side of the digital divide, but that does not mean they are fully digitally included. A student who only has a mobile phone to do homework will be at a disadvantage. While a mobile phone can connect to the internet, it may be slower, the screen is smaller and harder to see, and it is harder to type on it than on a full keyboard. Can you imagine typing a ten-page paper on a mobile device? That ten-page paper would also be difficult to write if a student does not have digital literacy skills. Someone who has a computer at home and fast broadband access but does not know how to use it would not be considered in a fully digitally inclusive position.

Angela Siefer, the director of the National Digital Inclusion Alliance said, "There are multiple Digital Divides, including home access, data caps, devices and digital literacy. And we will never close the digital divides. The goals within each digital divide keep moving. As technology changes, the goals move."

Homework Gap

Digital inclusion and the digital divide greatly affect students. Visualize two students just starting kindergarten. These students go to the same school and have parents that are supportive of their learning. The difference between the students is that one has high-speed broadband access and a computer at home, and the other does not.

In the beginning, the two students are at the same pace. They're learning their letters and numbers and how school works. But soon, their paths diverge. As they move up in school, more online homework is assigned, online content and etextbooks become mandatory to complete assignments, and their school may share grades and information to parents through email or other digital means. These changes affect outcomes.

One student can complete their homework at home on a desktop with a printer, while the other must complete assignments on a small cell phone screen. The student from the digitally inclusive home can regularly use the internet at home. The other student may need to go to the library and try to finish projects and homework in a specific window of time. One student has parents who can troubleshoot tech problems and help with questions. The other may have parents, who while they care about learning, lack the digital literacy skills to assist with homework.

This gap between the two students is called the "homework gap." While it begins in the early grades, it can persist through high school. According to a three-year study that examined outcomes between students in two elementary schools, one that had reliable high-speed access and the other that did not, students with more access had better educational outcomes. The student with broadband access at home is more likely to graduate high school, have higher grades, and be more digitally literate. While the two students started equally, their outcomes diverged. Those high school grades and skills can also affect college and career. While technology can bridge inequities, it can also exacerbate them.

CONNECTIVITY TRENDS

Connecting to the internet has come a long way since dial-up. Educators may remember the internet from their childhood. It was probably dial-up, which allowed only secure, immobile access to the internet. That connection took a while to boot up, access was not immediate, and if anyone in the house needed to use the phone, well, you might have to boot up and wait all over again.

Technology has improved connectivity exponentially. The concept of a "computer room" is foreign to Generation Z. Connectivity is instant and constant.

Trends are making that connectivity even more fast and ubiquitous. WiGig, or millimeter wave technology, promises to deliver speeds ten times faster than Wi-Fi. WiGig works with Wi-Fi, operating on a higher frequency with shorter waves. At WiGig speeds your hard drive can communicate in real time with your laptop sitting several feet away. The disadvantage of WiGig is that it can only work across short distances. However, with the growth of wearable tech, and people carrying several devices on their person at once, it promises to connect things even faster.

Another Wi-Fi technology that may revolutionize connectivity is Li-Fi. Li-Fi is a completely different type of transmission to Wi-Fi. Wi-Fi works through radio waves while Li-Fi transmits signals through light. Light waves are over 100 times faster than radio waves. So, the potential for (literally) lightning fast speeds is there. Pilot projects have been tested since 2015, but Li-Fi is not a commercially viable solution yet.

A technological change closer to the present is 5G technology, which is already being implemented. This 5G access works at a higher spectrum, above 60 GHz. A big reason 5G has been developed is to upgrade existing networks. As more devices and users need internet access, the current bandwidth can get crowded. With 5G, other frequencies and different antennae are used to minimize delays and give much faster speed.

Mobile Generation	Usage ID	The range of Frequencies; (Examples)	User Data Bandwidth (Practical examples)	Coverage per Antenna & usage
3G	Mobile	850MHz, 2100MHz	2-10 Mbps	50 – 150km Suburban, City, Rural area
4G	Mobile	750MHz, 850MHz, 2.1 GHz, 2.3GHz and 2.6GHz (Centimeter wave)	10-30 Mbps Long-Term Evolution (LTE) version	50 – 150km Suburban, City, Rural area
	Fixed Wireless		50-60 Mbps Long-Term Evolution (LTE) version	1 – 2km Home, office and high density area
5G	Mobile	3.6 GHz, 6 GHz	80-100 Mbps	50 – 80km Suburban, City, Rural area
	Fixed Wireless	24-86 GHz (Millimetre wave)	1-3Gbps	250 – 300 m Home, office and high density area

The summary of Frequency and data bandwidth: 3G to 5G cellular mobile generation
- 5G network real-world test: examples by Qualcomm's simulated 5G tests on Feb/2018

Figure 5.2. Frequencies and data bandwidth 3G to 5G. *Wikipedia Creative Commons*

If policy makers and educational administrators are making policies based on the "computer room" of their childhood, they are making false assumptions. Banning devices is not simple if Wi-Fi, or even Li-Fi, is a constant presence. How can you limit access when it's streaming incredibly faster everywhere you go? Those in charge must accept that access is fundamentally different, and what may have worked in 2005 does not work in 2015 and certainly not 2025. While this improved technology has promise to help connect more people faster, it still does not solve digital inclusion issues of literacy. That will increasingly be a need and a gap to be filled.

MOBILE TRENDS

A 2018 Pew Research study reports that 95 percent of teens have access to a smartphone. This is an increase from an earlier poll in 2014–2015 where about 75 percent of teens owned a mobile device. Mobile is king. Past trends and current trends have pushed mobile to the top and there's no indication that it will lose its throne soon.

In the future, 2016 may be remembered as a tipping point in technology. Since personal computers came to the market in the early 1980s, they have dominated the landscape. They were the only option for internet access for a generation. When mobile devices came onto the market they were not computers, they were actual phones. Early models in the late 1990s like the Nokia 6110 called and texted and offered simple games like the very popular Snake. That was all handheld phones could do at the time. While the internet was available, it wasn't until the mid-2000s that 3G technology improved enough to make it worthwhile to connect through a mobile device. Now many marketers and business owners define smartphones as a commodity. A commodity is a good or service which is widely available and needed. For example, oil is considered a commodity. With smartphones saturating the market and integrated into daily life, they can be seen as just as important, or even more important, than gas you would put in your car.

Then, on January 9, 2007, Steve Jobs, clothed in his famous black turtleneck and jeans, walked onto the stage of the Macworld convention and announced that later that year the first iPhone would be introduced. It came out on June 29, 2007. While the iPhone was not the first internet connected phone, its impact continues to be felt. That impact is largely because of the introduction of apps.

Mobile Apps

An app, short for "application," is simply a piece of software that can both run on a web browser or on a phone. One of the first apps was the game Snake, which was pre-loaded on Nokia phones. Apple did not truly invent the smartphone or the app. However, they changed and popularized these devices. As explained in Brian Merchant's *The One Device: The Secret History of the iPhone*, Steve Jobs fought with developers about apps. He wanted only Apple to develop the apps and didn't want third parties to get involved. Over time, Apple staff convinced him, and third parties could then create apps for the smartphone, but not without giving Apple a 30 percent cut to be on their Apple Store. This has been a huge profit machine for Apple and has allowed the app revolution to happen. App development became democratized. Small companies as well as large could have access to millions of eyes from the smartphone.

Apps are what makes a smartphone a *smart*phone. They also contribute to an increasing amount of screen time. The trends continue to show more and more apps being developed and downloaded. Statistica estimates total app downloads will leap to 352 billion in 2021. That's up from about 200 billion in 2017 which already was a jump from 2016, when there were about 149 billion app downloads. These numbers far exceed the number of people on the planet. If every person on the planet had a smartphone, they would need to download at least three apps to reach those 2017 numbers.

Who is downloading and spending the most time on those apps? Unsurprisingly, it's Generation Z. A company that measures cross-platform tech statistics, comScore, reports that people between the ages of eighteen and twenty-four report the most time on these apps, close to one hundred hours each month. These are the students in classrooms right now, who may have been born at the beginning of the app revolution and do not know anything different.

The app industry continues to be dominated by Google and Apple. These two tech behemoths have different strategies when it comes to apps. Apple has a curated store with higher restrictions to be accepted. In 2018, the number of apps in the Apple iOS App Store actually decreased, denoting a higher demand for quality. Google's Play Store focuses less on quality than quantity. The vetting process for a developer to be part of Google Play is less rigorous, and Google Play boasts significantly more apps. While apps were initially more of a democratic playing field, in recent years there are tighter controls and more competition. While more apps are being downloaded, trends suggest it will be harder for smaller companies and lone app developers to find an audience for their app.

Mobile Searching

Another trend in mobile are search engines. In 2015 comScore reported another significant mobile milestone. That was the year that more people accessed the Google search engine on a mobile device than on a desktop. This has an impact for advertisers, businesses, and other organizations. Already, people rarely go beyond the first page of search results. SEO Hacker estimates only 10 percent of people will go beyond the first page in a search. Mobile devices, with their smaller screen and more voice capability will probably bring that result down more. This has effects for media literacy, as will be covered in more detail later. What is popular is not always right.

Mobile searching is different from traditional searching. According to Think with Google, which reports on searching and trends for advertisers, about a third of people who are searching on their phone use location-based services. When you're out with your phone, where are you? You may be in a car, running errands. You want to find the information that is closest and fast. People search on their phones to find things close to them. Add Google Maps to a Google Search and people's interests, visits, and purchases may also be limited to that first page of search results. The days of driving around and finding unexpected serendipity are less common, or even desired, for younger generations.

Not only is the search different on a smartphone than on a desktop, the process itself can also be radically different. As opposed to typing on a desktop, when texting on a smartphone people are more likely to talk to the device. This is supported through voice-enabled apps, which encourage speaking rather than typing.

Marketers have said, and continue to say, that search engine optimization is vital for organizations wishing to reach people. Search engine optimization, or SEO, refers to building websites with the intent of staying prominent in search results through a variety of means. In addition to SEO, an organization might also need AEO or "answer engine optimization." People are finding things through their mouths, not their fingers.

In 2016, Google announced that 20 percent of searches on mobile devices were done through voice. While no newer statistics have been released as of this writing it's clear that a significant number of people are finding information in a fundamentally different way. With the growth in smart speakers, voice searching may become normalized and the primary process of finding information.

Mobile devices have changed user behaviors radically in about a decade. A generation is growing up not knowing anything different. The idea of searching on a desktop, playing Snake, having to track minutes on a data plan, and not having a computer in your pocket may become amusing relics.

SCREEN TIME

Estimate how many hours you are in front of a screen per day: 24 hours.

—Sarcastic response from a male eighth grader surveyed in 2018

American adults spend an increasing amount of time in front of a screen. In 2017, comScore reports the average amount of time was about two and a half hours a day. Those hours do not include work hours, just free time. Other reports, like Nielsen ratings, put that daily number over ten hours a day. Whatever the exact number of hours are, they have increased.

It's important to differentiate between screens. The term *screens* can include mobile devices, tablets, gaming consoles, TVs, and more. With some screens that hourly rate has decreased. TV use has declined. The marketing survey source comScore found that younger Millennials spend the greatest amount of time on mobile apps. Increasingly, accordingly to a Common Sense Media report, preschool age children are in front of a phone or a tablet rather than a TV.

An increase in screen time does not necessarily signify a problem. You can use a screen to research, or to cyberbully. You can use a screen to connect with family far away, or watch YouTube. Issues may arise with screen time based on the age and risk factors of the individual. Excessive screen time is a risk factor for problems, but it does not mean that it will cause the problem.

We ask our students who go through our digital citizenship program about their screen time. From our summer camps with adolescents in the summer of 2018 we found that 87.5 percent of students reported at least three hours of screen time. In our study, we asked them their most popular media platforms, and with the teens they were YouTube, Facebook, and Snapchat.

While more research is needed, we have found that there is a correlation between more screen time and a less digital citizenship knowledge and attitudes at the end of the class. Students who report more hours on a screen also have less knowledge of digital citizenship. This correlation could be due to several factors:

- Different attitudes toward technology than their peers
- Difficulties focusing in classes
- Frustration about being without a screen during the classes

Screen Time and Young Children

In 1999, the American Academy of Pediatrics (AAP) came out with a policy statement that recommended that "pediatricians should urge parents to avoid television for children under the age of two years." Many parents and practitioners interpreted this as saying no media exposure, but the AAP said this was not the intent. It has stood by its recommendation in an updated policy statement in 2016.

The new report provides new research in this area of hot debate. Educators, parents, the media, students, and others discuss such topics as what screen time is, how much of it is too much, and what type of screen time is acceptable. The research and debate continue, but a growing amount of research has come to more conclusions on the effects.

The updated 2016 AAP report notes the amount of change that has occurred since its earlier statement, stating, "Technologic innovation has transformed media and its role in the lives of infants and young children. More children, even in economically challenged households, are using newer digital technologies, such as interactive and mobile media, on a daily basis and continue to be the target of intense marketing." The report then gives specific recommendations, including this direct statement: "For children younger than 2 years, evidence for benefits of media is still limited, adult interaction with the child during media use is crucial, and there continues to be evidence of harm from excessive digital media use."

The growth of educational apps and the shrinking costs of tablets provide a device that can encourage interactivity, but it requires an invested adult. The AAP questions educational apps for young children and states, "Most apps also generally are not designed for a dual audience." This can be seen with YouTube, where there are few restrictions or policies to follow when labeling videos for children. ChuChu, an Indian company creating videos for young children, has grown rapidly in five years. The *Atlantic* reports that ChuChu has more than nineteen billion views on YouTube, compared to *Sesame Street*'s five billion. *Sesame Street* employs child therapists and educators and carefully creates content. Other app and content creators like ChuChu do not operate with the same level of rigor.

Excessive screen time can create health and developmental concerns in young children. The AAP reports research attaching excessive screen time to such risks as:

- obesity
- sleep problems
- decreases in parent-to-child interactions
- self-regulation problems
- cognitive delays
- social/emotional delays

These young children are in school or entering soon. They will take their screen time habits and viewing patterns with them.

Screen Time and Adolescents

A 2018 Pew Research study of teens found that 54 percent of teens spent too much time on their smartphone. In that study, most parents were concerned about this use, and they too struggled with disconnecting from their phone. Getting disconnected is difficult for teens. They have a screen in their pocket most of the day, their school may provide screens for learning and homework in their classes, and when they come home there are multiple devices: TVs, tablets, and more. It is not surprising that the report found that 45 percent of teens "are online on a near constant basis."

Currently, the National Institutes of Health is conducting a longitudinal study of over eleven thousand children. This ABCD, or Adolescent Brain Cognitive Development, study has some preliminary evidence on screen time. It found differences in the brains of some children who spend more than seven hours a day on smartphones, tablets, and video games. A researcher with the NIH, Dr. Gay Dowling, said that brain scans do show a thinning of the cortex in those children with lots of screen time, but the researchers don't know what this means, or if it's even harmful.

As with young children, more research is needed on screen-time effects. There are multiple risk factors that affect behavior. There have been associations between social media use and sleep disturbances in young adults as researched and reported in the journal *Preventative Medicine*. In 2018 the *Journal of the American Medical Association* found a correlation between excessive digital media use and symptoms of attention deficit hyperactivity disorder in teens. The connections between sleep, attention, and self-regulation will be explored later in this book.

The trends in screen time are shifting up for all ages, which necessitates a greater involvement from parents and educators to help create boundaries. The rules and boundaries that may have worked a decade ago are not effective with the shifting change of media consumption and availability. How to create those boundaries will be discussed in chapter 8.

GAMING TRENDS

I was a gamer when I was a kid. I spent many afternoons playing with friends gathered around the TV. But it was a different type of gaming. The biggest difference is the games had an end.

—*Story from the author*

Gaming has grown exponentially since the Atari 2600 black box came out in 1977. From square pixels to immersive virtual reality, the last generation has revolutionized the gaming industry and experience.

Young people love gaming. Statista, an online market research company, reports that over half of regular gamers are under thirty-five. Twenty-eight percent of identified gamers are under eighteen years old. While numbers have fluctuated over the years, males have a slight edge over game playing than females. In a typical classroom, around a third of students play regularly and educators can expect that when many of their students go home that day, they will go home to play games.

The way they play games, however, is different than it used to be. In about a decade, the gaming industry has shifted from the physical to the digital. Statista reports that in 2009 over 80 percent of video games sold were physical copies, but as with mobile access, that number shifted in 2016. Now most games are downloaded digitally. Digital games will only increase in the future.

Rather than the single physical game model, companies are shifting to a digital subscription. A gamer will purchase a monthly plan with downloads, rather than an individual game. A driving factor behind the subscription model is Steam. Developed by the Valve corporation, Steam offers servers, support, and digital rights management for PC gaming. Consider it like Google Play for PC games. The thought behind Steam and other subscription-based gaming is that players do not purchase games based on the company that released it, rather they buy the game.

The subscription model can benefit companies. With most games being digital, this model allows the company to push out updates to the games quicker. It also allows companies to create add-ons, like extra items or loot boxes that players can purchase in addition to the game. In the past, when a player would buy a new game, everything about that game came packed in a plastic case. Now a player purchases a code they input online, and if they want additional extras, a new area to explore, a new skin for their character, an additional character, they must pay to play.

Virtual Reality

Virtual reality (VR) is a simulated environment that provide a sensory experience that can include sight, touch, hearing, smell, and even taste. The term was coined in 1987 by Jaron Lanier, who founded the visual programming lab and made some of the first VR gear. The lack of technical know-how and processing speeds kept VR more of a niche hobby for many years. While Sega created a VR headset for the Sega Genesis in 1993, its cost and technical problems prohibited it from getting off the ground. It wasn't until the twenty-first century that the technology improved enough for commercialization, and not until the 2010s that the average person got involved.

Figure 5.3. Virtual reality headset. *Pixabay License*

According to Lucas Matney in *TechCrunch*, the turning point was in 2016. He writes, "After more than two years of heavy public hyping since Facebook's 2014 acquisition of Oculus for $2 billion, virtual reality is reaching an important turning point. VR has been promoted up and down the street and consumers seem to have grown oversaturated with all the media coverage of expensive tech that's inaccessible to them, but the platform is preparing for a mini-renaissance." Two years later, Matney's words came true. A plethora of new devices and games have been introduced since then, and the cost for headsets has decreased.

Statista estimates that the number of VR headsets installed will grow from seven million in 2016 to thirty-seven million in 2020. The headset market, once dominated by the Oculus Rift, now has new players, including Google's Daydream, HTC

Vive, Samsung's Gear VR, and the Sony PlayStation VR. Outside of headsets, the entire US industry of hardware and software is expected to reach more than $19 billion by 2020.

To go with those headsets, there are hundreds of games. The Samsung Gear and Oculus Rift allow access to over six hundred titles in the Oculus store. Valve, which dominates the video gaming streaming subscription market, also provides hundreds of games. In the past, limited selection, technical difficulties, and high prices inhibited popularization of this tech. That is no longer the case. VR is in every part of the gaming industry: PC, console, mobile games, and eSports, and it shows no sign of being a niche hobby anymore.

Virtual Reality beyond Gaming

VR is not just about gaming. Its applications go beyond play into entertainment, communication, education, and more. One application is 360-degree video. This type of recording uses multiple cameras in a single device. The user can view content from many angles by panning around and even looking up and down. YouTube is leading the charge and has many videos available for watching on VR headsets through an app. Hollywood is also getting more involved in VR entertainment. Production companies are exploring the new VR market, and one day instead of putting on 3-D glasses to see a movie, you may put on a headset.

Other 360-degree video content is found on Facebook. They offer a platform for users to share content, making social VR. Facebook has invested a lot of money and resources in recent years to create this immersive environment. They now offer their own VR headset, the Go. With this new tech, Facebook users can not only talk across continents, they can also interact with panoramic photos and 3-D objects.

Outside of entertainment and gaming, VR has applications in the medical field, which was an early adopter of VR. In 2016 at the Royal London Hospital, the first surgery was live-streamed using virtual reality. This allowed medical students and the public all around the world to experience surgery in real time. Physicians and researchers have also found success in using VR for children at the hospital, helping calm stressed-out patients and healing trauma victims.

That real-time application of VR in surgery has potential beyond medical science. While we can never truly get into someone else's brain and feel what others experience, VR gets us closer. An undersea welder could go under water without getting wet. A student could get a better idea of how a student in Australia lives. A soldier could experience war with no risk of injury.

VR presents opportunities for education, empathetic experiences, and a way to see the world. But like other new tech, it also presents yet another distraction that can occupy many hours and promote virtual experiences over real-life ones.

Electronic sports, also known as eSports or competitive gaming, is a fast-growing hobby and even a profession. Competitions have always been part of gaming, but as live-streaming and the audience for gaming have grown, eSports has moved from the living room to the stadium.

Over half of eSports fans are between ages eighteen and thirty-four and many teens make up the fan base. A typical eSport fan would be a thirty-three-year-old male who makes over $75,000 and has a child at home. These typical fans are highly engaged. Like a football fan who has a season pass and tailgates each home game, an eSport fan will spend a significant amount of time and even travel for games.

Fans aren't just spending time on eSports, they're spending money. It's estimated by Mindshare North America, a media and marketing agency, that expenditures on eSports will reach over $1 billion in 2019. Some of the biggest celebrity players in eSports make six figures. eSports is a growing part of the gaming landscape, and is not going away any time soon.

Mobile Gaming

What does a mobile app gamer look like? According to Think Google, which has tracked mobile gaming from the Google Play store, it is a thirty-six-year-old who plays their mobile game while waiting at the doctor's office. Mobile gaming, as opposed to other types of gaming, has a slightly older demographic. Seniors also enjoy mobile gaming; it's estimated about a quarter of seniors are mobile gamers. That's not to say young people aren't playing mobile games. But they are more likely to play on different platforms rather than mobile. Men and women play mobile games equally and for the same intention: to kill time. And they spend a lot of time killing time. Think Google estimates over an hour of game play each day on mobile apps.

There are a lot of people killing time. Statista reported in fall 2018 that gaming is the most popular category in the Apple iOS App Store. The Amazon AppStore also reports gaming as its most popular category and it is high in Google Play. Since the days of Nokia's Snake, mobile gaming continues to be a popular pastime, and trends suggest that the growth will continue. That growth is encouraged by profits. It's estimated by NewZoo that the global mobile gaming industry will increase 200 percent from 2014 to 2020. It's estimated that profits will exceed $72 billion in 2020. It is also the year that marketing and industry experts predict that mobile gaming will exceed all other types of gaming.

The increase of smartphone usage and the increase in availability of games will most definitely assure many more hours killed. Games will be just a fingertip away from playing.

Gaming Trends and Adult Expectations

"Why can't they get off their game?" This is a question many parents and educators may ask. But they must understand that the game this young person is playing is not the same type of game the adult played.

There are three main differences between game play with Generation Z and older generations:

1. Multiplayer options
2. Open-ended gaming
3. Availability and options

The physical model inhibits playing with other people. While as a child I could play videogames with other kids, they were in the same room. Now children and teens play with others living in other countries. While this does pose dangers, like cyberbullying, it also provides an immersive and appealing experience. Youth develop relationships and friendships with fellow gamers. Taking away a video game in the past meant that the gamer couldn't play a game. Now it means that the gamer can't play and they can't interact with friends.

Games now don't have an end. Popular massively multiplayer role-playing games (MMORPGs) like World of Warcraft (WoW) or Runescape are not designed to have a conclusion. Unlike previous games, where you may save the princess and the credits roll, an MMORPG will not stop. These games are set up for exploration, world-building, and meeting others. The point is the journey, not the destination.

Beyond MMORPGs, there are many other games designed without a destination. The extremely popular Minecraft is an example. In Minecraft the player builds, fights creepers and zombies, and plays with other gamers. You cannot *beat* Minecraft like you could Super Mario Brothers. Thus, an adult who is frustrated that a child may continue playing just one game must understand that one game will not stop. Games are less about accomplishment and skill than experience. While this may provide some valuable experiences for a player, it also increases the amount of screen time and decreases the time for non-gaming experiences.

There are many more options for game play for a member of Generation Z than Gen X. A player can pick from competitive sport games, mobile games, virtual reality, first-person shooter, and world-building games, and these games are continually updated and sent immediately to their device. It is harder to get away from games. You cannot just simply put them back in the box and set them in the closet. If the game is on your phone, which is constantly by your side, how can you put it away? There is always something new and shiny around the corner. For young people still developing self-control, simply shelving the game is not always realistic.

Understanding tech trends can be daunting; and while we can forecast, we simply do not know what will happen in the next five to ten years. In just a decade we had a mobile revolution, the gaming industry completely changed, broadband access spread across the world, and virtual reality became popularized. That is a small time frame for some big changes. For people working with youth, or anyone living in this type of fast change, an open mind is vital. In the twenty-first century the only thing that remains constant is change.

6

Teaching Digital Citizenship

Digital Communication and Media Literacy

The summer of 2018 I taught a class of elementary-aged refugee children about online communication. While English was not the first language for most children in the class, they had quickly picked up this new language and talked fluently to me and their classmates. Except for one student. This young girl only knew a few English words and had another girl sit with her who would explain and interpret the lessons. The English-speaking girl would be her friend's spokesperson, raising her hand to comment and ask questions whispered into her ear.

In this online communication class, we had an activity with emoji, those little icons that represent feelings, thoughts, activities, and much more. I asked the students to tell their life story with emoji. This girl who struggled to speak English, could speak emoji. She quickly filled up her worksheet with faces, hearts, and other icons. These pictures could transmit a complex story of coming to the United States, moving to a new home, and starting a new school. And that story could be understood by everyone in the class.

—Story by the author

Humans have always communicated. From gestures, grunts, drawings, knots on string, or impressions in clay, humans have a multitude of diverse ways to transmit messages. Communication is very, very old, but digital communication is new.

This chapter discusses two big elements of digital citizenship: digital etiquette and digital communication. It also covers media literacy and how technology is changing how we perceive, interpret, and find information. Two sample teaching activities on digital empathy and media literacy are included.

This chapter will explore that intersection of old and new. Digital communication trends will be discussed, as well as older research on psychology, the brain, and nonverbal communication. It will explain ways educators can better teach the ideas, history, rules, dangers, and opportunities of online communication in their organization.

WHY AND HOW DO WE COMMUNICATE?

The first text message was sent over twenty-six years ago. Since then, data from Apple and Android estimate that texts have multiplied to over 145 billion sent every day. In just a generation, huge changes in how we communicate have affected the whole world. However, changes in *why* we communicate remain the same.

We communicate to share needs, thoughts, and feelings with others. We send out that communication in the desire and hope that a receiver will connect, help, or understand us. The words that we use are basically symbols that represent certain things. Words are symbols, just likes memes, emoji, and text speak.

Unfortunately, symbols are often poor substitutes for the complex and always changing emotions and thoughts running through our brains. It is difficult to distill a contradictory thought like, "I care about you, but I'm very upset at what you did" in a symbol that can be understood by the receiver. Feelings are experienced on a spectrum. For example, people don't simply experience sadness—there is melancholy, wrenching depression, wistfulness, and much more that all fall under the umbrella of "sad."

In addition, we typically experience multiple emotions at once. Think of a parent sending their child off to college. It's both a beginning, and an ending. The parent is proud of their child, happy for their accomplishments, but they also feel sadness that their child is no longer a child, and even anxiety of them moving away. That feeling of pride, sadness, happiness, fear, and anxiety is hard enough to express in speech, let alone an emoji.

Nonverbal cues, like tone, gestures, facial expressions, and eye contact, can help transmit those complex thoughts into symbols that a receiver can decode. Humans are experts in nonverbal communication and are born hard-wired to be social creatures. Newborns immediately look and recognize faces around them and respond to other babies' cries and can pick out voices, even though they don't understand the words. Nonverbal cues provide additional channels for messages to be received and properly decoded.

Professor Albert Mehrabian created a communication model in the 1960s that examined how messages sent with nonverbal cues were interpreted. From his model, he found that 7 percent of messages were interpreted based on what the actual words spoken said. Thirty-eight percent of the messages the receiver heard were paralinguistic. This means that *38 percent of the messages from the words was received by the way the words were said*—only 7 percent was the actual words. Mehrabian's model found that facial expression communicated the most. Fifty-five percent of messages related to feelings and attitudes were transmitted through facial expression.

Think of a person who when questioned how they were doing crossed their arms, furrowed their eyebrows, and declared in a loud voice, "I'm not mad!" Would you believe the verbal message or the nonverbal one? While the words, "I'm not mad" are very direct, the overwhelming evidence of tone, body language, and facial expressions communicate an opposing viewpoint.

A word, gif, or emoji is limited in the different channels of communication it can share. A sentence in an email has a visual component; as opposed to communication in person, you cannot touch that sentence or hear that sentence. You cannot hear the pauses between words in that sentence, the pacing, loudness or softness, any lilt or any change in tone at the end of the sentence. The receiver of a written sentence is peering through a dirty window, trying to see what's on the other side.

Online communication is fast, efficient, and able to reach millions, even billions of people at once. However, it's a flawed channel of communication because it lacks tone, facial expression, body language, and all those cues that our human brains are wired for. Understanding how humans send and decode messages is vital for being an online communicator. While online communication will always be problematic, a person who carefully chooses words and the appropriate channels to send messages can prevent some messages from being misinterpreted.

Communication as Culture

Communication not only transmits feelings and needs, it also spreads culture. Every culture has its own slang, way of saying words, language, and more. The internet has its own culture, and each locale, whether it be an online forum, a website, a blog, or a game, has its own regional dialect. Media scholar Mark Deuze describes digital culture "as an emerging set of values, practices, and expectations regarding the way people (should) act and interact with the contemporary network society." Digital culture is shared through memes, FAQs, slang, text speak, GIFs, images, and emoji. It's not taught; there is no 4chan communications class available. To learn digital culture, you must experience it.

Digital culture is complex, and its many fiefdoms and territories each have their own narratives and speech. For adults working with youth, understanding digital culture may be frustrating.

Jocelyn Brewster, psychologist and founder of Digital Nutrition, sees that disconnect between adults and students in her practice. She said,

> Many adults have an attitude toward young people's technology use that is polarizing. For many there is a sense that they don't "get" young people's online worlds, the discreet and complex mechanisms within them, and why they're important. To some degree this is simply the "generation gap" at work, a sense of newness and difference, of change and loss of control that adults have as they notice youth cultures shifting rapidly in front of them.

Reactions from adults about this digital culture youth are engaged in can range from shaming to supporting. Educators may view teens communicating on Snapchat as trivial and may ban it in their classes. Or they may see it as a way the teens are encouraging social bonds and ask questions about it. Educators may view text emoji as a trend and something only young people do. Or they may view them as a valid method of communication and have a discussion on what those emoji mean.

Figure 6.1. Sleeping emoji. *Creative Commons*

In southern Utah there are stunning petroglyphs, which are images carved or incised in stone. The petroglyphs include depictions of landscape scenes, animals, people, and more. Many of these petroglyphs come from the Fremont people, who carved these symbols over one thousand years ago. In modern times these petroglyphs have been analyzed by academics and researchers, and they are highly respected and preserved. But at their core, they are symbols, just like emoji. Perhaps one day there will be researchers analyzing our digital communication with the same reverence as those long-ago petroglyphs.

Navigating digital culture is part of digital citizenship. Just as a foreigner to a new country must learn the customs and language to fully participate, a person must understand the customs and language of the internet to be an engaged digital citizen.

DIGITAL COMMUNICATION TRENDS

While the *whys* of communication have not changed, the *hows* have. Communication is more digital than face-to-face. While all ages are communicating digitally, it's adolescents who have jumped headlong into this digital world. A 2018 study from Pew Research had 45 percent of teens reporting that they were online "almost con-

Figure 6.2. Fremont petroglyphs. *Wikipedia Creative Commons*

stantly," which is double from the earlier Pew Research 2014–2015 survey. Between phones, games, speakers, tablets, texting, and tweets, an average young person's day is *filled* with digital communication. Trends in technology, education, and the way we work have influenced, and will continue to influence, the *hows* of communication.

Smartphone ownership has increased exponentially since 2007 with the introduction of the iPhone. Ownership has grown globally with Pew Research reporting 59 percent of adults own smartphones. That number is 77 percent in the United States and continues to grow.

In another Pew Research study, teens in the United States reported even higher numbers. Ninety-five percent of teenagers said they owned or had access to a smartphone. Having a universal communicator that is connected 24/7 has vastly contributed to the amount of digital communication. Previously, only an email could be sent from a wired computer, and speeds inhibited much more than written communication. But since the 2000s the barriers to digital communication have dropped. Why drive somewhere or arrange a face-to-face when it's easier to simply reach in your pocket to talk?

Digital Respons-Ability surveys almost all the students who go through our digital citizenship classes. One of the questions in that survey is what social media platforms they use. These surveys are from data collected from May 2017 to October 2018.

For students in grades seven to twelve, their top social media platforms are YouTube, Facebook, and Snapchat. Following those platforms teens reported Instagram as a favorite.

Some surveys specifically point to Facebook Messenger, not Facebook. In 2014 Facebook made Messenger a separate account, which allowed individuals without a Facebook account to use Messenger. Thus, when teens report Facebook as their second-favorite platform, they may be referring to Messenger.

For students in grades two to six, the top social media platforms are: YouTube and Snapchat. Following those two, younger students, like their older peers, report using Instagram and Facebook. Messenger Kids, a chat service Facebook created specifically for those under age thirteen, may be contributing to the growth of younger children reporting Facebook as their most popular platform.

Younger students were more likely to list a gaming platform like Fortnite or Roblox as their favorite social media platform. At first glance the game Fortnite does not seem like social media, but like most online games, there are chatting functions.

Across all grades surveyed, YouTube was consistently ranked as the most popular social media platform. Our findings are consistent with trends seen nationally. Pew Research reported in 2018 that the top three online platforms teens use besides Facebook are Instagram, YouTube, and Snapchat.

Another trend to watch is our increasing reliance on conversations with artificial intelligence. Communication is more likely than ever before in human history to be practiced not with another person, but with a machine. Since the smartphone, the only tech product that has grown as quickly is smart speakers, *Forbes* reported. They estimate that the number of smart speakers in homes will grow to over ninety million in 2020. Smart speakers are just part of the artificial intelligence (AI) communication market.

The most ubiquitous AI is the one living on our smart phones. This is why Siri owns about half the voice-assistant market. Siri came out on the iPhone early and Android products are still trying to catch up. While digital citizenship is focused on the human aspect, it's worth noting that young people are growing up communicating with the non-living. Perhaps a future edition of this book will have a chapter on digital communication titled, "How to Communicate Appropriately with Bots."

ISSUES WITH DIGITAL COMMUNICATION

Technology has made digital communication the easier choice. Broadband speeds have expanded. More devices are in homes and pockets. New software has provided more platforms and media to communicate by. And culturally, digital communication is more accepted and promoted than ever. There is a definite place for digital communication. It will not go away, and shows no signs of decreasing. But like with most things, there are pros and cons.

The table illustrates two sides to every issue. Technology is a tool and can be used for positive and negative reasons. For example, GoFundMe, a crowdsourced plat-

Table 6.1. Pros and Cons of Digital Communication

Pros	*Cons*
Fast and efficient	Can create silos of information that give a skewed sense of the world
Helps family and friends keep in touch over long distances	Digital relationships may come at sacrifice of other relationships
Inexpensive	Can be used for illegal purposes such as trafficking
Can be enjoyable and entertaining	Can distract from work, school, and other pursuits
Can provide flexibility in workplace arrangements	Can make expectations for work in personal time and places
Provides opportunities for people to learn about other cultures and beliefs	Is a medium for cyberbullying, trolling, and scams
Helps organize movements, plans, and people	Helps organize movements that incite violence and spread hate

form where people can donate to people and causes, has helped fund people from around the world. But that same platform can be used for nefarious means.

In November 2018, it was reported by the *New York Times* that a couple collected over $400,000 from well-wishers around the world for a scam they put together with a homeless man. Instead of using the money for its intended purpose, it was gambled and used to purchase expensive items. Another example is the alt-right, which uses platforms such as Gab, Reddit, and Twitter to organize hate movements. But those platforms have also been used to organize movements directly countering the alt-right.

It's important to remember there is a person behind the screen. Unfortunately, that person typically cannot be seen. Albert Mehrabian's research found that only about 10 percent of our messages through words are heard. Digital communication is a very flawed medium, which can exacerbate those cons.

An example of digital communication interpreted and misinterpreted, followed, commodified, and spread is the saga of #PlaneBae. In summer of 2018 on a flight from New York to Dallas, a woman switched seats with Rosey Blair. The woman ended up sitting in front of Rosey next to a man named Euan Holden. The two seatmates chatted throughout the flight, but did not know that Blair was quietly recording, photographing, and tweeting their entire interaction under the hashtag #PlaneBae. The tweets went viral, with many commenters eagerly awaiting the updates and others wanting their own #PlaneBae. Holden embraced the attention putting #PlaneBae on his Twitter profile. Blair was given corporate promotions such as a free flight from Alaska airlines. Brands stepped in offering products, and daytime talk shows called.

But then the other side of the story came out. For outsiders, reading the tweets and pictures painted a heartwarming story. But they were only seeing through the perspective of Blair, transmitted through the muddled waves of digital communication. The woman who sat next to Holden had an entirely different view of the situation. She issued a public statement.

Figure 6.3. Pictures from the #PlaneBae incident. ***Courtesy of the author***

> Without my knowledge or consent, other passengers photographed me and recorded my conversation with a seatmate. They posted images and recordings to social media and speculated unfairly about my private conduct. Since then, my personal information has been widely distributed online. Strangers publicly discussed my private life based on patently false information.

Readers of the story could only rely on an unreliable source. They could also not hear the tones of the interaction or the pacing. They, along with Blair, saw no facial expressions or eye contact. Yet despite this, decisions were made, attitudes and behaviors interpreted, and even action was taken. This happens constantly with communication. We assume motivations and behaviors of the transmitter of the message with little information. However, with digital communication we have even fewer clues and cues from the transmitter.

Another barrier to correct and appropriate digital communication is egocentrism. We assume that others share the same interpretations as we do. We cannot differentiate between our subjective reality and the outside world. Simply, we have an inability to completely understand a perspective other than our own. We cannot read minds.

Statistics support this explanation of egocentrism and our faulty brains. A study out of the *Journal of Personality and Social Psychology* found that people overestimate their ability to both convey their own proper tone and interpret others' tones over email. The people who read others' emails corrected the tone only slightly over half the time. Researchers theorized these results were because of egocentrism.

Everyone experiences egocentrism, although it's more prominent in childhood and adolescence. Adults continue to act and think egocentrically. For example, have you ever felt people are looking at you? Or that you're the only one in the room that feels nervous?

In the story of #PlaneBae the Twitter audience could not read the mind of Blair, Holden, or his female seatmate. Their brains jumped in egocentrically and made up stories and assumptions. The stories in people's heads went something like, *"This story seems like something out of a romantic comedy, I wish something like this would happen to me. These two seatmates must really like each other. I feel good when reading this story so I'm going to share it with others."*

Add our natural egocentrism, lack of nonverbal cues, our desire to connect, and technology together and you have viral information. Sometimes that information is positive and helpful, sometimes it's incorrect and harmful. Whatever type of information it is, our digital world has provided an unprecedented means to share it.

PREVENTION SCIENCE AND DIGITAL COMMUNICATION

The prevention science model can be used when addressing and teaching digital communication. Risk factors are situations, individual characteristics, community problems, and more that are more likely to create dysfunctional behavior. Protective factors do the opposite; they help mitigate or prevent that dysfunctional behavior from ever occurring.

What is dysfunctional digital communication? This question is subjective, but can include things like cyberbullying, trolling, lying online, sharing inappropriate content, cyberstalking, and more. Basically, dysfunctional digital communication is online communication that harms others. This behavior may be intentional, like cyberbullying, or unintentional, like believing something false and sharing misinformation. Some of these dysfunctional communication patterns will also be addressed in chapter 7 on online safety.

Communication, or the lack thereof, is a risk factor for multiple behaviors. The Centers for Disease Control lists scientifically proven risk and protective factors for a list of dysfunctional behaviors by youth. Table 6.2 shows risk factors that specifically relate to communication.

Table 6.2. Risk Factors for Dysfunctional Behavior

Risk Factor	*Dysfunctional Behavior*
Deficits in social cognitive or information-processing abilities	Violence
Antisocial beliefs and attitudes	Violence
Social rejection by peers	Violence
Isolation, a feeling of being cut off from other people	Suicide
Lack of empathy	Sexual Violence

Communication and connection are both risk factors and protective factors. Table 6.3 lists the protective factors that are connected to communication.

Table 6.3. Protective Factors for Dysfunctional Behavior

Protective Factor	*Dysfunctional Behavior*
Parental use of reasoning to resolve family conflict	Sexual violence
Emotional health and connectedness	Sexual violence
Empathy and concern for how one's actions affect others	Sexual violence
Family and community support (connectedness)	Suicide
Skills in problem solving, conflict resolution, and nonviolent ways of handling disputes	Suicide
Highly developed social skills/competencies	Violence
Connectedness to family or adults outside the family	Violence

Looking at these risk and protective factors, two common themes emerge. One is connectedness; connection to school, family, peers, adults not in the family, and one's own self. The other is empathy; having developed social skills to push through conflict and concern about others.

Technology is an amazing connection tool. It can connect individuals at any time of the day in any place instantaneously. Technology can be used to reinforce social bonds and keep connectedness over long distances. For example, a 2012 study out of Australia with refugees resettled in that country found that digital communication tools helped the newcomers stay connected to their family and country of origin. A 2013 study argues that adolescents provide a safe and important space to socially engage with their peers and can provide connection. However, there are opposing studies. One study in *Computers in Human Behavior* in 2009 found that internet technology leads to increased anxiety and depression. The research is mixed on technology's role in connection.

A 2018 literature review by Clark, Algoe, and Green in *Current Directions in Psychological Science* summarized those mixed results.

> Whether behavior on social network sites is good or bad for well-being depends on whether the behavior advances or thwarts innate human desires for acceptance and belonging. In other words, our interpersonal-connection-behaviors framework suggests that when social network use is focused on promoting connection, it is linked with positive outcomes; when it is not focused on promoting connection, its consequences are more complex.

The effects of digital communication depend on motivation and intent. The technology is not inherently good or bad. It's just a medium, a platform, and a tool.

> A sizable body of research has identified associations between the use of social network sites and lower well-being. Our framework suggests that negative consequences are likely to result from the use of social network sites when individuals engage in social networking behaviors that do not fulfill needs for acceptance and belonging. These behaviors are not new to these sites; instead, they can be understood as traditional pitfalls of social interaction within a novel context.

The medium of digital communication can make connectedness and empathy difficult. We miss out on tones, gestures, and the intricacies of conversation that can make connections deep. We cannot see the other person, may know nothing about them, so it can be difficult to feel concern for them. Difficult is not impossible, and there are ways to increase that empathy. One is through actively teaching it in the classroom. Research by Brewer and Kerslake has found that adolescents with lower empathy are more likely to cyberbully or be cyberbullied and that empathy-based interventions are suggested to address this dysfunctional behavior.

How do you teach empathy? That is a difficult question to answer because while you can impart knowledge of empathy, you cannot make a person *feel* empathetic. But, there are methods. Digital Respons-Ability has used this simple digital empathy activity with both adolescents and educators with positive results and feedback.

SAMPLE DIGITAL EMPATHY ACTIVITY

Materials: Class divided into small groups, six to twelve images online, paper or sticky notes, writing utensils

Instructions:

1. Share how information online can produce many different feelings. Explain how others may not react the same way to the same information.
2. Divide the class into small groups. Each member of the group needs a small stack of paper or sticky notes.
3. Show examples of online communication. This can be a meme, an Instagram screenshot, a Twitter exchange, texts, a GIF, or other. Pause after showing each image and ask the group to write down their initial feeling. Explain that there are no right or wrong answers.
4. After going through all the images, have the students compare their feelings with the feelings in their group.
5. Reconvene as a large group and go through the images again, asking different groups to share their thoughts. If desired, have them put their sticky notes on a wall or white board. You can designate parts of the wall/whiteboard as "Negative," "Neutral," or "Positive." Map out the different emotions on the board.

This activity was done in fall 2018 with a group of school counselors. In the small- and large-group discussion a wide variety of feelings were reported from the same image. A long discussion bubbled up from the crowd that led to the activity having to be cut short. One image used for the activity was from Wendy's restaurants.

Figure 6.4. Wendy's Twitter account roasting a user. ***Courtesy of the author***

Wendy's is known for their sarcastic Twitter feed that "roasts" followers and other organizations. They proudly participate in #NationalRoastDay and have followers regularly ask them to roast them. Some members of the class saw the roast as funny; others saw it as offensive and crass. When this Tweet was shown with teens, there was still a divided response, but a larger percentage of teens found it funny.

As with experiential learning, the real learning happened from self-reflection. This activity shows students very clearly that others may feel differently from the same stimuli. Understanding this fact combats our natural egocentrism and encourages empathy. Participants in this activity turn to their peers and ask, sometimes with very confused looks, "Why did you say that?" The instructor should make sure to provide equal time for different perspectives, calling on a variety of groups and people. Also, the instructor should make sure to reinforce that there is no right or wrong with the response and be careful not to share their own feelings so as to not influence the class.

When engaging in that digital empathy activity, here are some follow-up discussion questions to help the students internalize what they've learned, and push the discussion forward:

1. What example made you feel the best? Which one made you feel the worst? Why?
2. Does going online change your feelings? Or does it just reinforce them?
3. What are the benefits of talking online?
4. What are the benefits of talking in person?
5. Were there any responses from your classmates that surprised you? Why?

MEDIA LITERACY

Media literacy is the overarching term that describes an approach that teaches the application of critical thinking skills to media. It includes the ability to analyze, evaluate, and create media in all its forms and contexts. With the enormous growth of media in today's world, it's more important than ever and an essential part of digital communication.

Michelle Lipkin, the director of the National Association for Media Literacy Education sees the connection between digital citizenship and media literacy. "I have been heartened by the overlap between the media literacy and digital citizenship communities," she said. "It's super important that we work together because our goals—to ensure students are prepared to thrive in the media saturated world—align so nicely together."

That alignment is found not only in digital citizenship's element of digital communication, but also in digital etiquette, digital literacy, digital law, and digital rights and responsibilities. Media literacy is an older, more established practice that can be found in school subjects such as English, history, and even science and math. Any subject that utilizes external media channels can benefit from the approaches of media literacy. According to Lipkin, "concepts of media literacy originated many decades ago while digital citizenship is a really new concept."

Technology and Media Literacy

> *Just think of the way that, within a mere two decades, billions of people have come to entrust Google's search algorithm with one of the most important tasks of all: finding relevant and trustworthy information. As we rely more on Google for answers, our ability to locate information independently diminishes. Already today, "truth" is defined by the top results of a Google search.*
>
> —*Yuval Noah Harari*

Technology has changed media literacy not only because of the growth of media channels and their dissemination, but also because of *how* we find information and *who* is creating it. Much of that change comes from the algorithm. That algorithm can come from a search engine, a social media feed, a YouTube channel, a shopping site, or the many other digital interfaces we interact with daily.

Previously, a teacher may have taught a class basic media literacy concepts using the Who, What, When, and Where approach. A student would look at a media source and ask, "Who made this?" or "Where does this come from?" Those are still valid, important questions, but they make a big assumption—that an actual human created, shared, or curated the media source. Content has become more faceless, driven by data, not people. The answer to "Who made this?" may be "an artificial intelligence." And the response to "Where does this come from?" might be something like, "It comes from a foundation funded by an overseas organization who created bots to share their mission."

The answer to "Who created this?" becomes murkier with new machine-learning technology. For example, a deepfake is a machine-learning-generated image and/or video that can generate realistic results in a short time. There has been similar technology in the past; you may have seen it on a movie screen with CGI. CGI, or computer-generated imagery, uses 3-D computer graphics in special effects on TV, in movies, and in other video productions. Previously, this was an expensive and painstaking process involving many skilled programmers and artists. For example, the three *Hobbit* movies in 2012–2014 made the trilogy the most expensive back-to-back film production ever made. *The Hobbit* utilized CGI heavily through the Weta studio, making the estimated cost of the movies $623 million dollars.

In just a few short years, machine learning has greatly reduced the cost and time to make CGI. A person used to have to sit down at a computer and put in every single detail for every single millisecond of film. They would have to do calculations to make sure each hair moved in the right direction, the light reflecting off an image was accurate, and many more minuscule alterations to make a realistic image. Today, a computer can do most of those calculations. A person can now feed an algorithm many data sets and the computer generates an image and anticipates the next millisecond. It's more of an automatic process than manual.

Deepfakes appeared on the scene around 2017, with celebrity impersonations. The deepfakes found online are typically those of well-known figures because it takes a large quantity of data to generate them, and celebrities with hours of video are the best sources.

In addition to deepfakes, technology has made mimicking audio simpler. Artificial intelligence can better replicate human speech than ever before. Lyrebird, a software from Adobe, allows for someone to type in text, and have that text manipulated to a believable voice. Combining a deepfake with an AI-generated voice can make realistic videos to entertain, or trick. Students will have to delve further into "Who created this?" and perhaps should also ask, "Is this a human or AI?"

Algorithms have also influenced the *how* of media literacy. Previously, information was held by gatekeepers. The gatekeeping could be a sermon spoken in Latin, or books being chained to desks in the Middle Ages. Information was also held back through restrictions on who could go to school, or who was taught to read. In more modern times gatekeepers of information may have been the three main TV channels in the United States: NBC, CBS, and ABC. News was filtered through the news on just a few stations.

Perhaps you remember a time where information at a library was only accessed through a process of finding the reference in a card catalog, where then a librarian had to retrieve it. Today, the gatekeepers are algorithms. Instead of the priest or the government deciding what information you could have, an algorithm makes that decision—sometimes influenced by religion or government.

Gates in the past held back information, only letting a trickle out. Now gates let out information in a flood, and it can be overwhelming. That's why we rely on our non-human gatekeepers, algorithms, for that information. There's too much data and not enough time to wade through it. This is not inherently a good or bad thing, because algorithms are not good or bad. The person who created that algorithm may have nefarious intentions, but the algorithm does not have intentions or feelings or motivations. It simply performs its task.

We trust our algorithms more and more, not only because of the deluge of information we are confronted with every day, but because of our own lack of confidence and skills. We don't know the best way to find information, or we feel skeptical of that information. We may have never been taught media literacy, or we just have a minute to find something and want convenience over correctness. It is not wrong to rely on algorithms for information. They can retrieve information and process information much faster than our brains. But we should be wary of relying on them too much.

If we become used to desiring the quick and convenient choice, if we prefer to say "Alexa, how do I cook a turkey?" rather than trying to figure it out ourselves, we are denying ourselves alternative choices. Contrary to what smart speakers say, there is often more than one answer, and the top answer may not be the best. We sacrifice content for convenience and serendipity for speed.

If children grow up from infancy with answers at their fingertips, they may have less ability to think critically. They may have less patience for research and long-form reading. When those children become adults, they may simply accept the answer given by the algorithm and be influenced by the sometimes-malicious motivations behind the algorithm. Those future adults may have less confidence in their own abilities to find information and may adopt a naive acceptance of the top results of the algorithm, or a nihilistic distrust of all information.

Educators may be the only source of media literacy in a child's life. They may be a child's only exposure to some alternate viewpoints. But educators need to change and expand on how they teach media literacy education. Technology has changed how media is created, shared, and accessed. "Media literacy has never been more important," Michelle Lipkin said. "We are living in a 24/7 environment. If students are not prepared to thrive in this world, then we are failing them. We need to prepare them for the world they are going to be leading someday soon. We need to give them the skills to thrive."

Teaching Media Literacy

How can educators teach the important concepts of media literacy? First, organizations should realize that media literacy cannot just be covered in one subject. Media literacy encompasses more than language arts, it should be covered in all areas. A science teacher can discuss the process of peer review and why we should find science sources in peer-reviewed journals. A history teacher can examine bias and encourage students to consider perspectives outside their country's lens. Computer science educators can explain how algorithms can influence our ways of thinking. The 2019 Rowman and Littlefield series *Media, Marketing, and Me* also has resources for educators teaching these concepts.

"Media literacy is not meant to teach students *what* to think but rather *how* to think," Lipkin said. It's a lifelong process that encompasses school, work, and home. An individual who knows how to think can navigate the flood of information and examine algorithmic answers critically. Lipkin goes on to say, "The purpose of media literacy education is to help individuals of all ages develop the habits of inquiry and skills of expression that they need to be critical thinkers, effective communicators and active citizens in today's world." Being a digital citizen means being able to navigate the fast-moving waters of digital information and row a path independently of the flow.

A sample media literacy activity that supports digital citizenship is the "Are you in a bubble?" activity. A bubble of information can be described as an isolated way of getting and interpreting information. Algorithms support bubbles. We can now curate what information is sent to us; and that is a helpful and harmful thing. We can slow down the flow of information by changing preferences and settings, only visiting certain websites, or following certain influencers. This can help us disseminate a large flow of information, but we may inadvertently paddle to a deserted island.

That island may be comfortable, with everyone around us agreeing and sharing the same information, but it's isolated. Understanding our bubbles can help us critically examine our own biases, and the information we are exposed to.

The "Are You in a Bubble?" activity addresses our bubbles and the psychology behind them. When beginning the lesson, the concept of confirmation bias is introduced. Confirmation bias is a tendency to favor, interpret, search for, and remember information that supports our existing feelings, background, and culture. We all have our bubbles. Some of them were pushed on us through our family, our religion, or where we grew up. Bubbles can help us connect with others and feel part of the group, but they can also support misinformation and limit our critical thinking skills.

SAMPLE "ARE YOU IN A BUBBLE?" ACTIVITY

Materials: Paper and pencils, "Are You in a Bubble?" Reflection Worksheet

Note: The Reflection Worksheet can be found in appendix C.

Instructions:

1. Show the YouTube video "This Video Will Make you Angry" by CGP Grey.
2. Discuss confirmation bias and how we all have bubbles.
3. Have each student fill out the reflection worksheet and identify their own bubbles.
4. Discuss in either small groups or as a class after completing the reflection worksheet.

To encourage discussion and self-reflection consider asking these discussion questions after the completion of the reflection worksheet:

1. What could you do as an individual to make sure you didn't fall victim to confirmation bias?
2. According to a growing body of research, we tend to listen/look at/gather with those people who think/feel/see the world the way we do. In your opinion, is this good or bad? Is it useful or not?
3. Younger people tend to get much of their information from social media sources. Do you do that? Why? In your opinion is that good, bad, or neutral?

There are many sample lesson plans and activities for media literacy available. Lipkin said, "There is a growing community of media literacy educators that are a great resource for teachers. . . . An important thing that educators should know is that they don't have to start from scratch—there are tons of resources, organizations, [and] curriculum available for free."

Some resources for teaching media literacy include:

- NAMLE (namle.net) NAMLE has a listing of organizational partners with resources on their website.
- Media Smarts (mediasmarts.ca) This Canadian resource has research, activities, and more for digital and media literacy educators.
- KQED Education (kqed.org) This nonprofit focused on young people's multimedia education has professional tools and activities.
- News Literacy Project (newslit.org) The News Literacy Project is a national nonprofit that teaches students to be better consumers of news.
- Common Sense Education (commonsense.org/education) Common Sense Media has a toolkit for educators on news and media literacy.

Educators have a vital role in teaching digital communication. More information and conversations happen online than ever before. Understanding concepts of digital etiquette, digital communication, technology trends, and media literacy are needed for individuals to be participatory and knowledgeable digital citizens.

7

Teaching Digital Citizenship

Digital Safety and Security

> *If our current habits continue unchanged, it's easiest to map pessimistic and catastrophic scenarios. People will be surrounded by more misleading or false information, not less. We'll see more YouTube and Twitch stars testing the thresholds of what their audiences are willing to watch, which means ever more salacious, incendiary content, disturbing images and dangerous behaviors. . . .*
>
> *Our well-being is directly tied to our sense of safety and security, which would be upended in these scenarios. But the good news is that these scenarios haven't happened yet. We can decide that we want a different outcome, but that requires making serious changes in how we use and manage information today. . . . We can choose to improve the quality of our digital experiences by forcing ourselves to be more critical of the information we consume. . . .*
>
> *The world we see looking only through the lens of a single post never reveals all of the circumstances, context and detail. Schools must teach digital street smarts. . . . From an early age, kids should learn about bots and automatically generated content. They should have provocative ethics conversations—with their peers, not just their parents—about online content and about technology in general.*
>
> *—Amy Webb, quoted in "The Future of Well-Being in a Tech-Saturated World"*

There is a lot to be worried about around technology. There is not a day that goes by without a news headline of a data breach, digital sexual predator, or seeing negativity online. This fear is accelerated by the speed and constant flow of information. And we particularly worry about our young people. What are the effects of this negativity? Will they be safe? Will they make good choices?

Those fears influence our policy, parenting, and classroom decisions. There are reasons to fear—this tech is so new we don't know all the effects. There are no longitudinal studies because the tech hasn't been around long enough. However, making decisions when the brain is flooded with cortisol and adrenaline does not necessarily lead to the wisest choice. When we engage reactively, not proactively, with preventative matters, sometimes our choices make things worse.

Utah has one of the highest teen suicide rates in the nation. Suicide is the leading cause of death for young people aged ten to seventeen. In December 2017, the Utah Department of Health (UDOH) and the CDC published findings from an investigation of the suicide increase since 2011. They reported that 12.6 percent of decedents "had experienced a technology-related restriction prior to their death." While we certainly cannot be in the mind of the teen or parent in that type of crisis, that statistic suggests a reactive approach.

The adults working with this adolescent must feel overwhelmed, and they are trying their best to help. Witnessing negativity or cyberbullying happening through technology, it may seem a clear response to get rid of the device. The device seems to be causing the problem, and it may be contributing to it. But that device is a tool, and could be exacerbating risk factors, or be a protective factor. That device represents a lifeline to friends and community to some teens, as well as the place they experience loneliness.

Suicide is complicated with multiple risk factors and there is not one cause. But looking at that 12.6 percent statistic one has to wonder if the device being taken away was the last straw for that troubled adolescent. Are our concerns and fears around online safety and technology making it worse?

Technology has two sides. It's a lifeline and a contributor to loneliness. It's a place for facts and fiction. Unfortunately, the positive is easily overshadowed by the negative in the media. Jocelyn Brewster, Australian psychologist and Founder of Digital Nutrition, said, "Much of the media that gets traction does so because it is sensation or salacious. . . . Good news and positive stories about the everyday, mundane, and uneventful don't get covered the way the pathological or unusual do. There is no headline for the millions of kids who tonight will talk with their mates on social media, make a mediocre effort with their homework, and go to bed slightly later than they should have!"

This chapter will cover both sides of technology as it relates to the digital citizenship element of digital safety and security. It will cover the prevention science behind unsafe digital behaviors, the developmental stages of youth, and some strategies to help prevent the negative. Tough topics such as cyberbullying and digital sexual violence will be addressed. We will attempt to sort through the hyperbole, misinformation, and fear and dig into the "Whys" of online behavior to better create safer digital citizens.

DIGITAL SEXUAL VIOLENCE

A legitimate fear of caregivers and educators is digital sexual violence. This umbrella term can cover such actions as:

- privacy violations
- cyberstalking
- cyberbullying
- doxing, or sharing private information about someone
- unsolicited sharing of pornography
- posting shaming and other information or pictures without consent
- hacking and stealing personal images
- taking explicit pictures of videos without consent
- harassment, particularly with online gaming

Digital sexual violence can occur on many different platforms, including website comments, personal emails, social media, anonymous messaging boards, and dating apps. A Pew Research study in 2017 reported that men are slightly more likely to be harassed online, mainly through video games. Women are more likely to be *sexually* harassed online. Young women are particularly the recipients of sexual harassment. In that 2017 study, Pew research compared results from when they surveyed online harassment in 2014. They found an increase in harassment from all areas.

Part of the increase in harassment is not that people are crueler, but that it has become easier. Technology has created an anonymous means of engaging in one's darker impulses. A generation ago a young person most likely would share the family computer, probably in an open space. That computer would be slow and prone to disconnecting when someone wanted to make a phone call. A generation before that, there was no online harassment because there was no internet. Someone who wanted to engage in sexual violence had to take a hands-on, face-to-face, and non-anonymous contact approach.

There has always been sexual violence, but digital sexual violence is new. The internet did not create this violence, but it can propagate it. The anonymity, availability, and potential lack of consequences may influence people to externally act out their internal thoughts.

PORNOGRAPHY TRENDS

The internet has fundamentally changed our consumption and interests in pornography. Most people access pornography online. This consumption can include videos, online games, web cams, images shared over message boards or messaging services, and now virtual reality through a headset.

Pornography researcher Amber Morczek from the University of Washington tracked search trends from major pornography sites in 2004–2013 and found a growing trend of the type of pornography desired. The three pornography search words that grew the most during this time were "forced," "torture," and "rape scene."

Young people who have little understanding of sex, let alone pornography, may be confronted by a pornography very different from what the previous generation experienced. This type of consumption can influence patterns of thinking. Through the explosion of rape-oriented pornography, themes emerge. According to Morczek, these hetero-normative themes include the following:

- All women want sex from all men.
- Women enjoy all sex acts men desire and perform.
- Women who resist can be easily persuaded otherwise.

A literature review of adolescent pornography use found that those themes contributed to more adherence to gender-stereotypical beliefs, a higher likelihood to be sexually aggressive in boys, and a higher likelihood of being a victim of sexual aggression in girls.

Educators should be aware that pornography now is not simply topless pictures in a magazine, or a back-alley video store. It's an all-digital, 24/7-accessible platform that can contribute to unhealthy messages in young people about gender, sex, and consent.

Sextortion and Sex Trafficking

The nonprofit Thorn: Digital Defenders of Children partners with tech companies and law enforcement to target digital child abuse. They help identify child sex trafficking victims and child pornographers, and they educate young people about sextortion. Sextortion is the act of threatening another person to reveal intimate images or coerce them into doing something sexually they do not want to do. Typically, sextortion happens between people who know each other, and it's most likely a male sextorting the female. It may involve "catfishing" where an individual pretends to be someone else in order to solicit sexual pictures or videos. The perpetrator may know the victim from another place and use that personal information in some harmful way. According to Thorn, the average age of an adolescent's first sextortion experience is fifteen.

Sex trafficking is exploitation, like sextortion, but it is long-term abuse with different motivations. Sex traffickers exploit their victims for money, and the internet is the platform for that exchange. In a 2014 study, Thorn found 75 percent of sex trafficking survivors were advertised online, and the amount of face-to-face advertising on the street has decreased. Most victims of sex trafficking entered the life around age fourteen through strangers. Those younger than ten were typically raised from infancy for that life by family members.

Educators may have sex trafficking victims in their classrooms. The risk factors of victims of sex trafficking are being female, involved in child welfare such as living in foster care, being African American or Latino, being a refugee or immigrant, or identifying as LGBTQ. Youth who are sex trafficked are also more likely to be runaways or homeless.

A 2016 report by Brookings Center for Technology Innovation identifies risk factors of victims of sextortion. Seventy-one percent of victims are under eighteen, nearly all female. The perpetrators of sextortion are almost all male and are likely to be repeat offenders. Social media is involved in 91 percent of sextortion cases with minors.

Sextortion and sex trafficking are a new and growing concern and the legal system is still figuring out what's to be done. There is no federal law against sextortion, and some sex trafficking happens beyond international lines, making it hard to prosecute. In addition, the crime is underreported. A victim may feel ashamed for the behaviors they engaged in against their will, or that they were tricked by someone they trusted.

What can educators and caregivers do? Awareness is a first step; knowing that even though you may not see these crimes, they are happening.

Other recommendations for helping to prevent sextortion and sex trafficking include:

- **Create a safe space.** Victims who have an adult they can turn to are better off than those who keep those secrets. They need a place without judgment and shame to share what happened.
- **Victims should know they're not alone.** Many individuals have been a victim of sextortion or sex trafficking. It is not a moral failure on their part. In addition, most likely the perpetrator of that crime has had other victims, and by reporting and coming forward they can potentially save others.
- **Connect to support.** Recommend students to talk to a counselor, recommend a suicide hotline, and report to authorities. If a student is under eighteen, there may be mandatory reporting laws.
- **Do not save or forward images.** Educators should not save any nude or seminude pictures shared with them from minors because they could be liable for having child pornography. Minors also may be liable for legal consequences by forwarding pornographic images to others.
- **Know the resources.** The National Center for Missing and Exploited children has ways for students to make a report for law enforcement. Encourage students to report the images to tech companies, or take a screen shot if there is a disappearing image such as on Snapchat. Other resources include Love 146, which educates around trafficking and sextortion and a CyberTipline at missingkids.org.

Another preventative measure for digital sexual violence and other negative behaviors online is encouraging students to create their own emotional and time boundaries. When children understand their own emotions and feelings and can step back and say, "I feel uncomfortable with this," they are more likely to say no or get an adult involved.

It's easier to set boundaries when you've practiced them first. In an emotional or tense situation, cortisol may flood the brain, making it harder to say no. A sample activity done with elementary-aged students helps the students learn the appropriateness of boundaries and involves role-playing them.

SAMPLE BOUNDARIES ACTIVITY

See appendix D for "Types of Nos."
Materials: Create a sheet with "Types of Nos" or write them on the board
Instructions:

1. Introduce the students to the concept of saying No. Help them understand that saying no is important when you're feeling uncomfortable and overwhelmed.
2. Introduce youth to the first type of No. Discuss when/how they might use it.
3. Divide students into groups and have them discuss in their groups when/how they may use the other types of Nos.
4. As a class, discuss what they learned about Nos and boundaries.

Sample Discussion Questions for Setting Boundaries:

- Why is it important to understand the different types of no?
- Does telling a person no mean that you are giving up?
- Does telling a person no mean that you do not like them?
- When is it not okay to say no?

CYBERBULLYING

I was doing a meme activity with high schoolers around ways to be positive online. Memes are those images, cartoons, and GIFs with pithy, sarcastic, funny sayings shared online. We were creating physical memes with templates of images: landscapes, pets, and people. I asked the students to write a caption on the images to make their meme. What's something inspirational they could write on the picture to put in their locker? Is there a positive note they could write on their meme to give to a friend? The students got to work in small groups, captioning their memes with small sharpies—except for one group in the corner. This group was huddled over whispering and I approached.

"How is it going?" I asked.

> *The oldest boy in the group looked at me and said, "This is dumb. Memes aren't like this."*
> *"What are memes like?"*
> *"They're supposed to be a joke, make fun of stuff," he said.*
> *"What do they make fun of?"*
> *"Stupid people."*
> *I asked, "Why would you want to make fun of stupid people?"*
> *"Because it's fun. It's just a joke. We all do it. I don't know why people get so uptight about bullying."*

That teen hit on something that was lacking in the discussion of cyberbullying that often takes place in adults-only spaces. Cyberbullying is not always what we think it is. There's evidence to back up his assertion. A study of middle and high school students published in the *American Journal of Orthopsychiatry* reported that 40 percent of students who cyberbully say they do not experience any feelings of guilt or shame. In the study, some of those students reported that online bullying made them feel better. They said they felt "funny, popular, and powerful" online. The researchers wrote, "We believe that competition for status and esteem represents one reason behind peer cyberbullying."

Cyberbullying is not a black-and-white issue. The victims are the perpetrators and the perpetrators are victims. This subject is also complicated because it's multidisciplinary. Clark, Algoe, and Green described this problem.

> Many studies have been conducted on Facebook and other social network sites, but to date, no single theoretical perspective has organized the literature on the association of social network sites with well-being. . . .
>
> This fragmentation is understandable in light of the fact that this literature arose across disciplinary boundaries, guided by concepts that emerged from different theoretical backgrounds. Difficulties in using experimental designs to assess causality in this domain also present challenges for testing any overarching theory linking use of social network sites and well-being. These issues, however, do not mean that past research cannot be conceptually integrated. Social network sites appeal to their users because humans are social creatures who require connection with others to thrive (Baumeister & Leary, 1995; Leary & Baumeister, 2000), and these sites help people meet this basic need. However, the same social risks that abound in everyday life also abound on social network sites.

Disciplines such as education, psychology, technology, youth development, and more all are affected by cyberbullying. But each discipline has its own biases, frameworks, and perspectives. Digital citizenship, with its multiple approaches and industries working in the same space, also is susceptible to the same biases. This has led to confusion on the topic of cyberbullying. This section will dive more into the research of cyberbullying and offer a sample activity for educators.

Why Do We Cyberbully?

There's a narrative that's said in schools and households.

"Oh, they're just jealous of you"
"Just ignore those mean girls"
"He's just sad and lonely and that's why he says those things"

There's truth in all of those statements, but they miss the whole picture. These statements are also made to comfort the victim at the expense of the bully. When we label someone, calling them "mean" or "jealous," we create distance between ourselves and that individual. That distance preserves our own feelings, but it does not create any empathy.

Cyberbullying is complicated and there are numerous reasons for it. The reasons go beyond bullies = bad and victims = good. A review of the research identifies both individual reasons and motivations related to peer and social groups.

Reasons and motivations for cyberbullying:

- loneliness
- access and opportunity
- jealously
- to feel funny and powerful
- competition for status in peer groups
- hurt and resentment after a breakup
- victim of cyberbullying
- boredom

Looking at the list, the narrative that bullies are always bad becomes murky. People who cyberbully don't necessarily bother others online because they are out to hurt or be malicious. They may cyberbully as a coping mechanism because it makes them feel good, or just because they have nothing else to do.

Bullying vs. Cyberbullying

Society has always had bullying. Traditional bullying or bullying that happens outside of a digital medium is our model for cyberbullying. But traditional bullying and cyberbullying are different.

There are different types of traditional bullying, which include verbal, social, and physical bullying. Bullying is also defined by repeated behaviors. These behaviors include:

- sexual harassment
- teasing
- threats

- public embarrassment
- leaving someone out
- hitting or kicking
- breaking someone's personal property
- spitting or biting
- aggressive and rude hand gestures

StopBullying.gov, the official bullying prevention website of the United States government, discusses traditional bullying through the perspective of power. "Kids who bully use their power—such as physical strength, access to embarrassing information, or popularity—to control or harm others." There is a power imbalance to traditional bullying. According to a 2017 report on Youth Health by the Centers for Disease Control and Prevention (CDC), traditional bullies are most likely to be male because of a difference in strength and because males can have more access to power. But with cyberbullying there is not always a power differential.

Cyberbullying democratizes bullying. People who may not have access to power through popularity, physical strength, or social capital can engage in bullying behaviors with less risk. A small student wanting to stand up to large upperclassmen would most likely stay away. But the internet allows that smaller student to push back against their classmate online without as much risk of physical altercation.

That's not to say that cyberbullying flips the traditional bullying model on its head. But through non-physical means, and anonymity, it opens up the space for bullying behaviors to individuals that might not have engaged in it otherwise.

The teen in the meme story described himself as a "loser," but on the internet he can be anyone. He can be funny and powerful through sharing memes online. He can get back at what he perceives as unfair treatment to him. This is not an excuse for negative behavior online, but an explanation. And using the old narrative of bullies = bad ignores students who are disenfranchised or rejected.

Marginalized and disenfranchised students, while they may have more access to push back against power, are, like with traditional bullying, most likely to be victims. That CDC report found that those who are at highest risk for high school cyberbullying are those students who have the least access to power.

The most likely victim would be an LGBTQ+ ninth grade girl. In the social ecosystem of a high school, this student is not at the top. Being female, having a sexuality that is not of the majority, and being younger, puts her at risk. The report found that girls are more likely to be both perpetrators and victims of cyberbullying.

Policy responses to cyberbullying are, unfortunately, similar to traditional bullying. Schools in all fifty states and in other countries have enacted zero tolerance policies related to school discipline and bullying. Zero tolerance is an approach that enacts strict regulations and bans against certain behaviors and items. Students are always punished for breaking these regulations. In the case of bullying, a school enforcing a zero-tolerance policy would immediately punish the perpetrator. A student who hit another would be suspended or expelled, and a student who cyberbullied may have the same fate.

There is no evidence that zero-tolerance school policies reduce drug abuse and violence. In fact, according to Welch and Payne in "Zero Tolerance School Policies" (2018), a review of these policies found that zero-tolerance policies had "unintended consequences, such as alarming disparities that negatively affect poor and minority students." The authors go on to say that "ample evidence suggests wide-ranging harm to students, school, and communities."

Adopting a zero-tolerance policy to both bullying and cyberbullying behaviors may make parents and school administrators feel better. And they may seem better; the perpetrator may be expelled or suspended, and those behaviors may stop. However, the behaviors did not stop because the problem was solved, but because the circumstances changed. That short-term solution may have long-term consequences for the perpetrator, who very likely was also a victim and marginalized, and is now being isolated from peers, school, and community.

Strategies to Combat Cyberbullying

There are positive and pro-social strategies to combat cyberbullying. StopBullying.gov recommends preventing school bullying by teaching students about bullying, offering evidence-based programs, and training staff on what bullying is, what the policies are, and engaging staff, parents, and administrators to create buy-in.

A research-driven and peer-reviewed approach to preventing bullying is Positive Behavioral Interventions and Supports (PBIS). PBIS is a school-wide approach that addresses strategies based on prevention science to define behaviors, collect data, define consequences, and monitor students, linking academic and behavioral performance and connecting behaviors at school to home. It's not a one-size-fits-all approach with a clearly defined set of rules, because people are complicated. Schools that implement PBIS are found to reduce bullying incidents. Resources and help funded by the US Department of Education can be found at https://www.pbis.org.

On an individual level, one strategy is not shaming. Students may not feel any guilt from cyberbullying; in fact, they may feel like cyberbullying is the right thing to do. If a student doesn't believe the behavior is hurtful and an adult or other authority figure comes in and blames and shames that behavior, the student will not listen. If you don't feel like you did anything wrong, and someone tells you otherwise, your immediate responsive is most likely defensive and anger. You will not be in a place where you can listen or engage in any self-reflection.

Before instructing or enforcing rules and policies, students need to understand the whys. Why is that behavior hurtful? Why does the school have that policy? One way to share the whys is to have consistent rules. If students feel like the rules are not being applied equally, they are less likely to follow them. If students feel like a teacher or other adult is not being held to the same standard as those rules, they may not comply. For example, if a rule in my home was to always put the dirty dishes in the sink after eating, but then my child saw me time and time again leave my dishes at the table, that rule becomes confusing and unfair. Why should they follow a rule that I don't have to follow?

Empathy is another answer to cyberbullying that helps get to the heart of the whys. A 2018 study out of Frontiers in Psychology found that when empathy was activated, it encouraged cyberbullying to intervene. When the research subjects could understand what the people on the other side of the screen might be experiencing, they spoke up and got involved. If a student can grasp that a certain behavior, even though it may seem funny and make the student feel powerful, has real-world impacts, it can help foster self-reflection and possibly stop future cyberbullying.

Prevention Science and Cyberbullying

Prevention science has a great deal of application to the complicated subject of cyberbullying. If an educator can identify the risk factors in students, and encourage protective factors, they can potentially stop cyberbullying from occurring. A review of research around violence, cyberbullying, and traditional bullying identifies the risk and protective factors.

Risk factors will evolve with age and circumstances. Some risk factors, like intergenerational poverty, racism, and sexism are particularly hard to overcome with protective factors. These societal and historical problems will not go away.

Bullying is another problem that will always be here. As long as there are people and peer groups, there will be bullying. But just because the risk factors are large and long-standing, does not mean prevention cannot happen. Prevention science engages multitiered strategies involving caregivers, individuals, and systems.

Table 7.1. Risk and Protective Factors for Bullying

Risk Factor	*Protective Factor*
Lack of empathy	Ability to feel empathy toward others
Mental Illness	Access to mental health treatments
Lack of coping skills when dealing with losses like a break-up	Effective coping skills
Unsupervised and unrestricted access to the internet	Afterschool programs and/or pro-social activities to fill up unsupervised hours
Boredom	Hobbies, activities with peers
Lack of sleep	Strict bedtimes at home, later school start times, no technology in the bedroom, medical interventions
Victim of cyberbullying	Support from others and quick response by authority figures from cyberbullying
Member of a marginalized community	Support community environment of accepting differences

Prevention is one person, one task, and one step at a time. Educators have a great opportunity to target individuals to help them develop narratives, thinking strategies, coping skills, and self-regulation to deal with the pernicious and long-standing problems of society. One small step that educators can take to prevent cyberbullying is the LAST Technique.

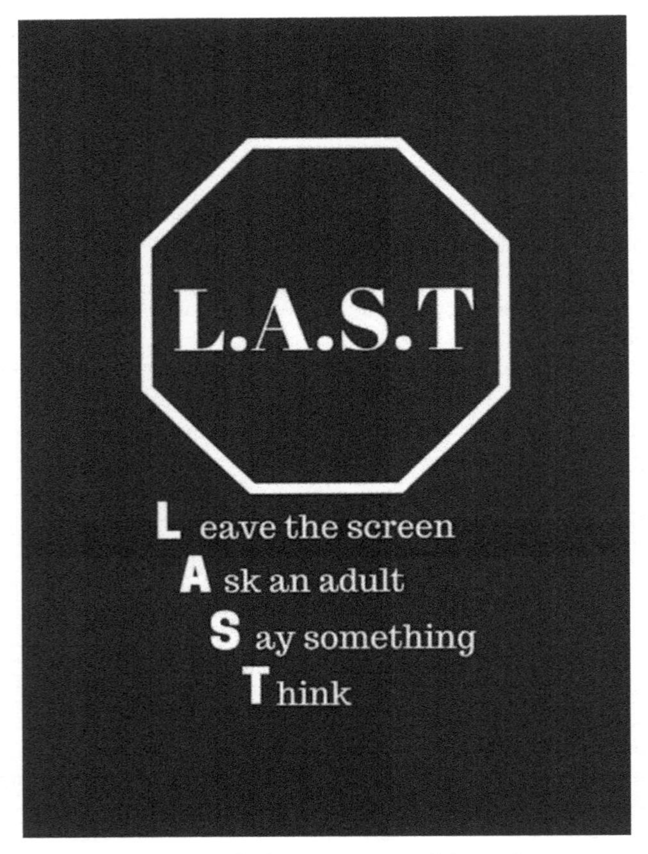

Figure 7.1. LAST Technique. ***Courtesy of the author***

The LAST technique was developed by Digital Respons-Ability in response to a risk factor with cyberbullying: unsupervised and unrestricted access to the internet. It's aimed at young children in grade three and below. At those ages, children are not likely to seek out inappropriate content online. They typically don't have the context, desire, or vocabulary to look for pornography or violent content. And they are less likely to be in romantic relationships with peers or in competition with them. When these children are exposed to inappropriate content or cyberbullying, it is often by accident. Children come across that content using a sibling's phone, at a public computer, or on their parent's tablet.

The LAST technique is an easy-to-remember strategy for those children when they encounter such content.

SAMPLE LAST DISCUSSION

Materials: Whiteboard, markers, eraser
Instructions:

1. Write on the board:
   L: Leave the Screen
   A: Ask an adult
   S: Say Something
   T: Think
2. Go through the LAST steps with the children and discuss them. Tell them that if they see something that makes them scared, worried, or uncomfortable, the first thing they can do is leave the screen. Empower them to feel like they can set their own boundaries. Afterward, they can ask an adult to come look at what they found. Say something about what they saw. Tell the students that even after they show an adult, they may need to tell somebody else. Not all adults will listen, unfortunately. Tell the students that they can also talk to their parent or guardian.
3. Discuss ways to report websites. Some sites like YouTube and Facebook have a button that you can report what you saw.
4. After talking about showing an adult, tell the children to think about what caused that website or image to show on the screen. This is not to blame the children but to make them self-reflect.

Questions for Discussing the T: Think

- Did someone put that content there?
- Were you using someone else's computer or phone?
- Did you click on a picture or screen that changed the website?
- How did it make you feel?

Educators and parents want their children to feel safe online. There are dangers there. With sextortion, cyberbullying, pornography, and more, you may feel a high sense of fear and anxiety. That's understandable and normal. But when we're afraid, we don't always make the best decisions. Online safety is complicated. It's not black-and-white. There are motivations, both malicious and positive, that people do what they do online. Understanding those human motivations can help us prevent issues and address online safety. There's always a person behind the screen.

8

Teaching Digital Citizenship

Digital Health and Wellness

I was at a meeting with school counselors a while ago where the conversation turned to the Dark Web. There was a case in a local school district where a student had purchased a gun off the Dark Web, another one purchased drugs. The counselors were concerned. One asked me earnestly, "What can we do? How can we stop kids from getting on the Dark Web?" I gave them what I'm sure was an unsatisfactory response. "There's not a lot you can do. Yes, there are red flags parents and educators can watch for, but at the end of the day, if students decide to get on the Dark Web, you can't stop them."

—Story from the author

The frustrations and concerns of those school counselors are understandable. They want to protect their students and they are fearful about what's online. Parents and teachers experience those same feelings. We are constantly reading in media reports about some abduction, cyberbullying, or other negative incidents. We want to believe in fail-safe solutions. We want to believe that if we do A, B will happen. But those beliefs and feelings, while understandable, leave out something very important: free will.

A young person should be able to make their own decisions, even bad ones. They should be allowed to make mistakes—even if those mistakes are harmful. That's not to say educators and parents should not engage in preventative measures—but ultimately, young people will decide their path.

Digital health and wellness, an element of digital citizenship, concerns an individual's choices on how to engage with technology. Digital health involves social and emotional learning skills. It has a close intersection with psychology and prevention science. Through work with students and research into behavioral psychology, two main concepts emerge when teaching digital health and wellness: self-efficacy and self-regulation.

Ultimately individuals will make their own choices with their health, but if educators can encourage self-efficacy and self-regulation, they will help create a path to healthier choices and a better chance at long-term satisfaction. This chapter will focus on digital health as it relates to those two psychological concepts with research-based solutions and practical activities to incorporate in a classroom.

WHAT IS DIGITAL HEALTH AND WELLNESS?

Digital health and wellness can mean different things to different people. With the growth of wearable tech, some people see it as a way to become more physically healthy. It can also mean dealing with digital distractions, like not texting while driving. To others, digital health is synonymous with online safety, avoiding physical and psychological harm.

What often comes to mind with digital health is hours in front of a screen. Screen time in particular has become a hotly debated topic. Increasingly, people see digital health as limiting technology in as many ways as possible. In October 2018, Nellie Bowles with the *New York Times* wrote an article called "The Digital Gap between Rich and Poor Kids Is Not What We Expected." In the piece, Bowles describes a movement among rich parents who are banning screens, while lower-income students have more screen time. "It wasn't long ago that the worry was that rich students would have access to the internet earlier, gaining tech skills and creating a digital divide. . . . But now, as Silicon Valley's parents increasingly panic over the impact screens have on their children and move toward screen-free lifestyles, worries over a new digital divide are rising."

Digital health does not just mean one thing, it's a holistic approach. Just like digital citizenship is incomplete if it only covers one element, digital health is not effective without a broader discussion of the way technology can both positively and negatively affect physical and emotional health. Psychologist Jocelyn Brewster of Digital Nutrition said,

> I really think we have only just started to explore this. There is a lot of work to do on what "healthy" even means when it comes to this and the danger of overemphasizing "goodness" over "realness." There are lots of great academics who explore many of the issues of authenticity and young people online that need to be given oxygen, over the folks (who have great intentions) who decide to take up some kind of cross to bear against technology and "protecting" kids, rather than working with them in a meaningful way.

A companion piece to the *New York Times* article reported about child care contracts that expressly forbid phones, or screen-free private schools. Parents and educators are taking more extreme measures to "protect children."

The media discussions around digital health focus less on working with the child around technology than creating rules and contracts to limit the child's access. There is research supporting limited screen time. The American Academy of Pediatrics has reservations about screen time under age two. But the discussions on screen time are across all ages, and they are spoken with a sense of fear and anxiety.

When our brains are scared and awash in cortisol and adrenaline, we don't always make the best long-term decisions. Our decisions are on the short term: "my child is having a tantrum, so the device gets taken away." Or, "I'm having problems with the students focusing on this online research project, so I'm going to change the assignment." Those solutions may address the immediate behavioral issues in the short term, but they do not teach the long-term social and emotional learning skills to truly be digitally healthy.

Self-Efficacy

Self-efficacy is the belief that one can achieve one's goals. It affects all types of human behavior. Psychologist Albert Bandura, who created the theoretical construct of self-efficacy, said that people with high self-efficacy are more likely to view hard tasks as something to be mastered rather than avoided. Those with higher self-efficacy are also more motivated to complete tasks, and if they fail, they'll ascribe that failure to external factors rather than blaming themselves.

The online environment provides countless and constant choices that individuals must make. For a student some of those choices might be:

- Should I finish my homework now or watch this video?
- Should I get off Instagram even if it's making me feel down?
- Should I create this game, or just play a game?
- Should I keep texting friends, or visit with my family?

If individuals believe that they are in control of their choices, their fate, their tasks, then they are less likely to be swayed by distractions and the many alternative choices online. They will see themselves as in control of the device, not as being controlled by it. They can use technology to do their homework, research online, create something difficult, rather than move to tasks that are easier and more fun. People with high self-efficacy have higher self-control and self-confidence, and the more they master new skills and projects, the more they believe in their ability to achieve.

Self-efficacy is hard to teach. You gain it by doing, not listening to others. But by instruction students in some healthier thought patterns and strategies, educators can push them to try and show them that they are ultimately in control.

When parents and educators try to push their own definition of digital health onto students, they are not encouraging self-efficacy. Students have to make the choice to be digitally healthy. They have to create their own plans and strategies.

An activity that Digital Respons-Ability has done with adolescents demonstrates the encouragement of self-efficacy. This activity encourages healthy sleep patterns. Lack of sleep is a risk factor for a host of negative behaviors. When adolescents, who are already lacking in sleep, have their sleep disrupted by technology it can lead to mental health issues and other problems.

The activity involves a lesson where the class shares facts around the blue light emitted from screens and how that affects melatonin production. Students are encouraged to map out their own sleep cycles and a circadian rhythm is described. After the information is shared, and students self-reflect on when they are most awake and sleepiest, the class creates their own game plan.

SAMPLE SELF-EFFICACY ACTIVITY

See appendix E for the Sleep Plan Worksheet
Materials: Your Sleep Plan Worksheet, pen or pencils
Instructions:

1. After discussing the effects of technology on sleep and having the students map out their own sleep patterns, introduce the concept of healthy habits around bedtime and waking.
2. Pass out your Sleep Plan Worksheet
3. Go over the worksheet. Offer suggestions on how to sleep and wake up better (i.e., have a dark, quiet, cool room. Eat an hour before bed. Let light in the room when you wake up.)
4. Allow each student to create a personal bedtime and wake-up plan using the worksheet.
5. Have the students share their game plans with their neighbors.

Sample Discussion Questions for Self-Efficacy Activity

- What would be a simple change you could create now to help you sleep and wake up?
- How do you feel at school when you're sleepy?
- Why do you think that American society fails to encourage healthy sleep habits?

Not once in that activity does the educator tell the student what to do. The teacher offers the facts, suggests options, and encourages the students to make the choices. When discussing those healthy sleep and waking habits, the language used is not "right" and "wrong" but "good" and "better."

I did this activity once with a group of teen girls. As they completed their worksheet, I could hear them talking to each other. This group of girls were close—they would text late into most nights. But they recognized that they were tired at school.

After they completed the worksheet, they told me that they decided that instead of texting late at night, they would text in the morning. This would help them wake up and go to bed earlier. That group of girls had self-efficacy. They believed they could

Figure 8.1. Activity mapping out sleep cycles. ***Courtesy of the author***

accomplish that goal, and they proactively moved toward it. I could have lectured that group, shared scary stories about lack of sleep, talked about long-term consequences, and told them what to do. But that would not have been nearly as effective as encouraging and empowering the students to make their own choices.

SELF-REGULATION AND TECHNOLOGY

In addition to self-efficacy, another key component for long-term healthy engagement with technology is self-regulation. Self-regulation, sometimes termed as self-control or willpower, is an essential skill for learning development. The concept is found across disciplines, in clinical psychology, developmental psychology, addiction research, and more. Different disciplines use different words to describe the concept such as: grit, inhibitory control, working memory, persistence, and the ability to suppress thoughts and work through distractions.

Self-regulation, which originates out of your prefrontal cortex, is the behavioral ability to make decisions in your long-term interest, consistent with what you truly believe. Unlike other mammals, humans can avoid distractions and forecast the future; we do not have to immediately respond to all the stimuli and impulses. Emotionally, self-regulation is the ability to calm yourself down when you feel upset and cheer yourself up when you're depressed.

Having self-regulation is a protective factor that can help predict developmental outcomes throughout one's life. A 2014 study in *Child Development* found that low self-regulation in kindergartners predicted more conflict with teachers, less school engagement, and overall less success in older grades. One study found that children who had strong attention skills in kindergarten or first grade were more likely to graduate from high school, despite socioeconomic backgrounds. Another study of young children found that those with stronger self-regulatory skills were 50 percent more likely to graduate college by age twenty-five.

Self-regulation can be affected by trauma, stress, temperament, and family environment. A famous study known as the "Marshmallow Test" out of Stanford in the 1960s and 1970s tested children's self-regulation. The children were told that they could eat a marshmallow now or wait fifteen minutes and receive another one. Those children were tracked as they aged and those who waited the fifteen minutes were found to have better life outcomes such as higher rates of graduation. However, when this study was replicated with a larger sample size there was a clear finding that economic background was the factor, rather than self-control.

It was theorized from those outcomes that children who grew up in poverty, and could not anticipate a future meal, had an adaptive response to the marshmallow. Might as well eat what's in front of you because you don't know when you'll get it again.

Technology is like offering a chocolate covered marshmallow in the study described above. Technology offers entertainment, novelty, and social connections, and it is constantly available. It's a hard distraction to ignore, and even harder if one is lacking in self-control. Technology can exacerbate the desire to procrastinate and make learning a struggle. A study out of the University of Nebraska-Lincoln studied over seven hundred students across six US universities about their digital habits in the classroom. More than 80 percent of the student respondents reported that digital devices caused them to pay less attention in the class and miss instruction.

Digital citizens must be able to sift through constant stimuli online. They need to look through the distractions and focus intently on the task at hand. Digital citizens must also be able to sit with negative feelings, self-reflect, and respond appropriately. They need to look at the long-term, even when they are feeling bored, frustrated, angry, or upset online.

Even young people who are lacking in self-regulation can work to develop it. Self-control can be encouraged at home or in the classroom. One way to promote self-regulation is by modeling healthy habits.

Educators and parents have a great opportunity to model self-control as it relates to technology. Digital Nutrition founder Jocelyn Brewster comments, "Educators and adults generally would benefit from checking in on their own habits and how their use of technology sends a range of signals to young people, about what is acceptable in terms of when, where and why they choose to use their phones/devices and how young people sometimes might have to 'compete' with the device and online activities for their parent/caregivers attention."

When educators ask their students to put away their devices and focus but then the teachers pull out their own phone, this causes a mixed signal. Parents who talk negatively about "screen time" but don't hold themselves to the same standards as their young children, are setting themselves up for a scenario with their now-preteen children calling them "hypocrites" and refusing to listen.

Developing self-control starts young, and it is influenced by the adults in a child's life. Some self-reflective questions an educator can ask are:

- How often am I on a screen in the classroom?
- Am I patient when waiting for something? Do I ever interrupt or hurry along my students?
- Are my classroom policies clear about digital distractions?
- When am I pulling out my phone? What am I feeling when I check it?

Another way to encourage self-control is by giving young people alternate choices when they do inevitably experience boredom or frustration. A generation ago, a bored student might write a note to a classmate. Now it's a text message. Earlier, a teen whose attention drifted would doodle in a notebook. Now that teen looks at a YouTube video. Both the past and present scenarios are examples where the student is trying to self-regulate, to feel comfortable in the space.

We all self-regulate. It's normal. However, as we age, we learn to self-regulate in ways that are less distracting to others and ourselves.

A phone is a device for distraction; however, it is so distracting that it can inhibit other processes. For example, more states have passed hands-free phone laws due to increasing research on how much a phone in a car distracts the driver. A white paper from the National Safety Council considers driving with a cell phone a "serious public threat." It summarized over thirty research studies on driver performance and found that the act of "attention switching" when using the phone overloaded the brain, juggled focus and attention, and affected reaction time.

When students pick up their phone in class, it's very difficult for their brains to both listen to the instructor and pay attention to the phone. However, there are alternatives for distraction that can not only encourage learning in class, but help students develop healthier habits for self-regulation.

One suggestion is doodling. In student classes taught by Digital Respons-Ability, teens are given a distraction booklet with coloring and doodling activities that support the curriculum. We have found that it helps them participate more in discussions, stay off their phone, and participate.

Figure 8.2. Distraction journals created by Digital Respons-Ability. ***Courtesy of the author***

Beyond anecdotal experiences of students benefiting from doodling, there's scientific research. A 2009 study by psychologist Jackie Andrade found that individuals who doodled recalled 29 percent more information than those who did not. The reasoning is that boredom or frustration activates the brain's limbic system and things like doodling or fidgeting are an effort for the brain to stay awake and alert. Having permission to fidget or doodle keeps your brain attentive longer.

Doodling is just one method to encourage self-regulation. Other ideas are offering fidget toys. Every time Digital Respons-Ability teaches a class we bring a fidget box. In that box are items such as:

- Rubik's cubes
- Squishy balls
- Silly putty

- Soft miniature stuffed animals
- Magnetic fidget toys
- Metal brain teasers

Students have the option of looking in the box and self-selecting what toy they want to use. Typically, the students identify their favorite toy early on and continue to use it in most classes. We tell the students that they can doodle and fidget all they want, but to try not to pull out their phones. For teens, it can be a challenge to put it away, but by offering a substitute, they're more likely to set it aside.

Self-regulation is a skill that must be developed and practiced over the lifetime. It's not easy, especially with notifications, pings, beeps, rings, and more, but mastering brings long-term learning success.

Prevention Science, Self-Regulation, and Self-Efficacy

Numerous benefits of self-regulation and self-efficacy have been explained in this section. How do those benefits align with the prevention science model? What is the potential risk in behavior and outcomes for students lacking in self-regulation and self-efficacy?

The Centers for Disease Control and Prevention (CDC) lists attention deficits and poor behavioral control as risk factors for perpetrating youth violence. This violence does not have to be physical. Students who struggle to control their behavior may overreact when seeing something online, and lash out through cyberbullying or trolling.

Self-efficacy works as a protective factor with bullying. A 2013 study in *Social Development* found that students who believed they had the ability to develop positive friendships, coped with being bullied better. "Close friendships inform adolescents of their value, as well as provide support and emotional resources during stressful events," the article states. Self-efficacy around social relationships is a self-replicating protective factor. People who believe they can make and keep friends are more likely to make and keep friends, and then that makes them feel more valued, giving them the confidence to develop even more relationships.

The risk factor of impulsive or aggressive tendencies is also a risk factor for youth suicide. A child that is prone to act without long-term planning or thinking is more likely to carry out a suicide threat. Another risk factor for suicide is a feeling of hopelessness. Not believing you have the capacity to accomplish your goals or to have self-efficacy can lapse into believing that there's no use in trying.

Parents may think that their child's feelings of hopelessness are coming from the child being on the phone a great deal. The solution in the adult's mind may be to just take the device away. But feelings of hopelessness or feeling out of control do not arise from the tech tool; they come from a mix of cultural, social, genetic, and biological traits.

A student who grew up in poverty may develop deep feelings of insecurity about safety, security, and food. That feeling of scarcity may come out in behaviors online. The student does not want to put the device away or have it taken away in a classroom because it represents safety, something that is a personal possession and asset. A student who has ADHD, whose brain struggles with focusing on the task at hand, may act out in class in an attempt to focus, not to be disobedient. A student who has experienced childhood trauma may develop a deep distrust of adult figures, and may react strongly when an adult figure tries to enforce technology restrictions.

Developing self-efficacy and self-control will be harder for students who have grown up in adverse circumstances, or whose brains work differently. It's also hard for educators, balancing the various needs, personalities, and behaviors in a classroom. But understanding and sympathizing that not all students will react to technology the same way can help teachers reach those students, and administrators develop inclusive policies.

MINDFULNESS AND MEDITATION

Too much of the education system orients students toward becoming better thinkers, but there is almost no focus on our capacity to pay attention and cultivate awareness.

—Jon Kabat-Zinn, creator of mindfulness-based stress reduction

Mindfulness and meditation are practices that can encourage protective factors in individuals and create digital citizens. Mindfulness is the practice of paying nonjudgmental, purposeful attention to the present. The ability to critically think, focus, pay attention, self-reflect, communicate, and listen are vital skills for safely and proactively navigating the digital world. These practices can be easily added to a classroom's or home's daily routine and can have effects beyond digital citizenship into other subjects and areas of life.

Anna Smyth is a mindfulness instructor and has worked with students and educators to incorporate the practice in their classrooms. She finds mindfulness particularly important with all the distractions in the modern world.

> Our lives are filled with distractions. Every waking moment, many things are competing for our attention. This constant hum of stimuli and distraction leads to exhaustion and poor mental and physical health. Mindfulness is a practice which, if done regularly, helps us in two primary ways. First, we cultivate a deep sense of nonjudgmental awareness. Without changing or "fixing" anything, we simply begin to notice just how distracted and agitated our minds actually are every moment. Second, when we are more aware of ourselves in the present moment, we can start to be more deliberate with our attention and choices. We begin to live our lives more present and focused.

Technology does not encourage mindfulness. It's difficult to have deep, slow thinking with information flying at you quickly. Smyth finds mindfulness a help with the problematic platforms of tech.

> Technology like many other things can be a very dangerous weapon or a very useful tool. The difference simply depends on the user's choices. . . . These technology platforms are not inherently dangerous or damaging to our health; it's the way we engage with them that is problematic and mindfulness can help. For example, it's very common for someone to reach for their phone and scroll through a social media feed for no other reason than to assuage a feeling of loneliness or anxiety. What research is showing, however, is that social media usually exacerbates those uncomfortable feelings rather than making them go away. Most of the time we're not even aware that the reason we're grabbing a device is to avoid loneliness or some other uncomfortable feeling. However, if we bring mindfulness to our encounters with technology, we start to see and understand our motivations much clearer. Mindful awareness helps us notice when we are engaging with technology for healthy reasons versus unhealthy ones.

Research behind Mindfulness Practice

There is an increasing amount of research on the mental and physical health benefits of mindfulness. A study with MRI scans reported in *Scientific American* shows that after an eight-week course of practicing mindfulness, the amygdala, or "fight-or-flight" center of the brain shrinks. This early region of the brain, part of the limbic system, is associated with fear and stress. If the amygdala shrinks, the prefrontal cortex, the part of the brain associated with executive functions, long-term plans, and self-regulation becomes thicker.

Trauma and continuous stress put a brain's amygdala on high alert. This affects a person's ability to look beyond to the future. The amygdala's goal is for safety and survival, to get out or fight. It's an appropriate response to a physical threat, like those our human ancestors faced continually in the wild. With a release of cortisol and adrenaline, our brains pushed us to run away, or fight, so we could live another day. Unfortunately, our brain struggles to differentiate between an immediate physical threat and a non-immediate trivial one. Being attacked online elicits a response from our amygdala similar to being attacked by a tiger.

Over time, those constant stresses and perceived threats affect our day-to-day lives. We may struggle to concentrate and sleep, find ourselves irritable and aggressive, and fail to empathize and listen to others. A small slight can turn into a big argument. Or a pop quiz turns into a mountainous test of endurance.

Mindfulness helps our primitive limbic system calm down, and our executive functions of the brain take over. A 2015 study reported in *Developmental Psychology* with preschool children who took a twelve-week mindfulness-based Kindness Curriculum in a public-school setting found an increase in executive functions, like self-regulation. The American Psychological Association (APA) reports another study about how mindfulness affected participants to focus attention and ignore distractions. A group of experienced mindfulness meditators were tested against a control group and the experienced group "had significantly better performance on all measures of attention."

Other studies reported by the APA found mindfulness meditation decreases impulsivity. It helped individuals step back from an emotionally traumatic image and get back to focusing on the task at hand. The internet is full of such images that can invade your screen and mental space. The ability to step back and reflect is valuable to navigate and focus. Mindfulness has also been found to have physical benefits such as better immune functioning and lower blood pressure.

"Key aspects of emotional regulation such as being aware of and accurately identifying emotions as well as appropriately responding to them are core outcomes of mindfulness practice," says Anna Smyth. "Central tenets of any mindfulness practice are to (1) be aware of whatever is happening in this moment and (2) refrain from judgment or reaction. A regular mindfulness practice can be particularly useful for youth whose emotional regulation skills have just recently come online and, like a child that has recently learned to walk, they aren't quite yet as stable as adults in these skills."

There are an increasing amount of organizations bringing mindfulness to their curriculum and routines. Corporate America has been bringing mindfulness classes into lunch breaks. Schools have been incorporating yoga and mindfulness in P.E. And more parents are teaching mindfulness techniques to their children. As the distractions and stressful content proliferates online, mindfulness and meditation can prove a bulwark against that rushing tide.

Incorporating Mindfulness and Meditation in the Classroom

Mindfulness is not an activity that needs to take a lot of time or money. By incorporating simple and short techniques, educators can encourage a lifelong practice in their students and reap some of the mental and physical benefits in behavior. Mindfulness is something that can be started at any age. Anna Smyth suggests, "Developing a mindfulness practice as a child can have great long-term benefits. Establishing the habit at an early age may increase the likelihood of maintaining the practice . . . into adulthood."

Adolescents are particularly in need of mindfulness practice. They have more risk factors for being victims of cyberbullying or digital sexual bullying and are dealing with lots of physical changes in their bodies. Smyth says, "According to the American Psychological Association's 2014 report, teens are the most stressed-out age group in the US. A personal mindfulness practice can act as a protective health factor for youth to cope with stress and related issues like anxiety, insomnia, eating disorders, and so on."

In chapter 7 the LAST technique was described as a response to risk factors with cyberbullying. This technique is targeted to young children grades three and below. Part of the benefits of LAST is that it utilizes mindfulness as a way for children to stop and reflect on a situation where they may see inappropriate content online.

Along with the LAST technique, Anna Smyth, mindfulness educator, suggests the STOP Practice. "The S.T.O.P. practice is well-known within the mindfulness community as an accessible technique for youth and adults alike. Parents can practice the technique together with their children to foster trust, acceptance, and support the development of their children's emotional regulation." STOP includes the following steps:

S: Stop what you're doing (both in the mind and body)
T: Take a deep breath
O: Observe what's going on (around you and inside of you)
P: Proceed

STOP can help students take a break and clear their mind when they encounter something uncomfortable. That pause can be enough for them to calm their emotions and react appropriately.

Mindfulness is part of Digital Respons-Ability's student curriculum, with different techniques being used for children and teens. The children's mindfulness techniques typically involve more movement, like walking around or wiggling. With the teens there is less movement and more reflection.

One popular meditation used in the mindfulness community is Five Senses Meditation. It involves using the five senses: sight, hearing, touch, smell, and taste. It's been adapted for the classroom where there would most likely not be food.

SAMPLE MEDITATION ACTIVITY: FOUR SENSES MEDITATION

Materials: None
Instruction:

1. Introduce the students to the concept of mindfulness and meditation
2. Speak and/or write on a board the components of Four Senses Meditation:
   See four things
   Hear three things
   Touch two things
   Smell one thing

3. Conduct the meditation slowly. Afterward ask the students how they felt after the meditation. What did they see, hear, touch, and smell?

Discussion Questions

- Have any of you ever meditated before? If so, what do you do?
- How can mindfulness and meditation help you when you're stressed? When you need to sleep? When you're upset?

There are more mindfulness resources than ever for educators. However, Smyth cautions using just any curricula. "Mindfulness as a professional industry has exploded over the last ten years with a vast market of books, certifications, and accrediting institutions. However, the credibility of these resources unfortunately varies widely and can be extremely difficult to navigate for an educator with both limited exposure and time to research the best options."

There are several research-based mindfulness curricula and resources Smyth would recommend:

- **Learning to Breath (L2B):** "Learning to Breathe is an evidence-based, age-appropriate mindfulness curriculum that has received support from the US Department of Education as well as the Collaborative for Academic, Social and Emotional Learning (CASEL) which listed L2B as one of only four mindfulness programs that meet the research criteria for effective social and emotional learning," Smyth points out.
- **Mindful Schools:** This resource offers online courses for educators and can also reward continuing education credits.
- **Mindfulness-Based Stress Reduction (MBSR):** This is an eight-week course that teaches mindfulness experientially in a group setting.
- **Mindfulness Journal:** This journal is peer reviewed and has the latest research on mindfulness.
- **Center for Mindfulness:** The University of Massachusetts Medical Center is where Jon Kabat-Zinn first established a mindfulness research community. Since 1979 it has been offering training, research, and support online and in person.
- **Mindfulness in Education Network:** Offers a network of close to two thousand educators to support bringing mindfulness in the classroom.
- ***Trauma-Sensitive Mindfulness* by David Treleaven** is a book that goes into the harm that can result if individuals with trauma are instructed by a teacher who is not trauma-informed and offers adaptive practices for trauma survivors.

Anna Smyth recommends involving the entire school in mindfulness practice. "Some schools and districts in the US have established initiatives that require all educators as well as key administrators to be trained by qualified professionals using evidence-based curricula. . . . This is the most sustainable approach. If students, educators, parents, and communities are all practicing mindfulness regularly, the likelihood of positive outcomes—both short and long-term—increases substantially."

Perhaps in the future when someone goes into get their physical exam, the doctor will not only check blood pressure, but online activity. Digital health affects physical health. And someone's emotional and physical health affects their digital health. As people's lives become more intertwined with their online lives, the need for more prevention and intervention practices will increase. Parents, educators, and students should all engage in regular digital health checkups for long-term happiness and success.

9

Teaching Digital Citizenship

Digital Commerce, Digital Law, and Digital Rights and Responsibilities

Teaching digital citizenship should be a holistic process that looks at digital behavior from multiple perspectives with knowledge from several disciplines. This book has worked to cover as many perspectives as possible and all the knowledge areas. Digital citizenship has nine elements:

1. digital access
2. digital literacy
3. digital communication
4. digital etiquette
5. digital law
6. digital rights and responsibilities
7. digital health
8. digital safety and security
9. digital commerce

This chapter will address the elements not previously covered: digital commerce, digital law, and digital rights and responsibilities. To be a full digital citizen, an individual must understand all nine. You can't have digital etiquette without digital communications skills. Without understanding digital literacy concepts, a student will struggle to be safe online. For a media-literate student, all the elements are intertwined.

DIGITAL COMMERCE

According to a 2017 U.S. Bank survey, 47 percent of those asked said they preferred the use of digital apps to make payments versus cash. Broken down into age groups, the cohort preferring digital payments the most were Millennials aged nineteen to thirty-six. Those preferences are continuing to grow, and the landscape of purchasing and payment, already revolutionized by the internet, will continue to change.

Digital commerce is the use of the online marketplace. It can include being a savvy buyer or seller, understanding what means of digital payments are out there, evaluating prices and reviews, and differentiating between real and fake financial scams. One way to describe digital commerce is three intersecting literacies: media literacy, financial literacy, and digital literacy.

Digital commerce is even more important now because of the growth of fintech, or financial technology. Fintech is new technology that changes and automates financial services. Fintech initially was built for the back end of financial institutions, but much of the growth has been for services for consumers. Fintech can include anything from borrowing, lending, banking, fundraising, investments, and wealth management.

According to a report by Statista in 2018, most financial transactions and banking services are conducted online throughout the world. An individual who does not understand how these transactions work; know how to utilize fintech services; and evaluate prices, services, and products will not only be more likely to lose money, but also career prospects.

Mobile payments are on the rise, particularly among young people. A study from financial tech analyst Juniper Research said that by 2012 over three billion users will access banking services through digital devices.

While these mobile payment apps are not supposed to be used by those under age eighteen, many younger people can get around that requirement by clicking a box. In addition, some companies target younger people, as with Snapcash, used on Snapchat, which is disproportionately used by minors.

There are pros and cons with using these apps. They are convenient and fast. However, students should also know there are hidden fees and scams out there.

Some popular P2P (peer-to-peer) payment apps include:

- Venmo
- Zelle
- Cash
- Snapcash
- Apple Pay Cash
- PayPal
- Facebook Messenger
- Google Pay Send

Many students do not get any financial literacy education in school. The Chaplain College Center for Financial Literacy had a 2017 report card on financial literacy efforts in schools in the United States. That report shared the startling fact that most states do not require any financial literacy education. In addition, only five states across the nation received an "A" for financial literacy education. There is already a lack of media literacy instruction and digital literacy teaching in classrooms. Although some students may have qualified media specialists with time in class and specific digital literacy instruction or may have teachers that are passionate and educated on these topics, many students may be woefully unprepared after they hit eighteen and are starting careers, setting up their own bank accounts, and being deluged by credit card offers.

If students are already not receiving basic financial literacy skills, they are certainly not getting much at all on fintech. Travis Cook, who is the financial literacy coordinator for the Utah State Board of Education, says that K–12 education typically does not incorporate any fintech in their curriculum. Colleges struggle too. Cook reports that colleges are scrambling to keep up with the changing and fast-paced fintech industry.

Financial Scams

The ecommerce and fintech landscapes have several landmines. The anonymity of the internet, plus the ease with which personal and credit card information can be stolen, has encouraged a proliferation of scams. Adolescents are particularly vulnerable to scams online, as they may lack financial, media, or digital literacy and are also at a stage in their lives where they are highly influenced by peers and want to fit in.

Some financial scams include:

- **Fraudulent money transfers.** Since email was invented there have been scams to try to convince people to wire their money. It may be someone pretending to be a bank that needs your personal information or a distant relative from another country who wants to share their inheritance with you. The scenarios change, but the goal is the same, to steal money. Wire transfers are hard to reverse, which is why they are popular for scam artists. P2P apps like Venmo are a new medium for this scam. A fake buyer contacts a seller online about an item. The seller asks for payment and the buyer has money transferred over the app. However, a day after the transfer is approved, the buyer cancels the transaction and keeps the money but takes the seller's item. Apps typically take two to three days before the money can be withdrawn and transferred to the other account, allowing an opportunity for these fraudulent buyers to cancel the transfer.
- **Charity scams.** Charity scams create up a fake organization or story to solicit donations. These pop up particularly around a crisis, taking advantage of people's desire to help. These types of scams have been found on crowdfunding sites like GoFundMe. Social media has also allowed an easy way for scam artists

to reach a wider audience. Scammers may post that they or someone they love has cancer and needs money, or may solicit money to send to a charity, but then pocket all or part of those donations.

- **Data breaches.** Anyone who makes purchases online is vulnerable to a data breach. These can occur to a person or a company and involve sensitive data being stolen, viewed, shared, and/or copied. These are becoming common occurrences. In a December 2018 article, *Business Insider* noted, "It seems like every week, a new company has to notify its customers that their data may have been compromised, and personal information may have been affected." In 2018 there were large data breaches with Marriott hotels, Google, T-Mobile, Facebook, MyFitnessPal, and many more. Unfortunately, in the situation with corporate breaches, there is not a lot a consumer can do. But students can understand that they have to be wary about what information they share with companies, and get in the habit of monitoring their credit and accounts.

A very popular online scam that young people may be particularly susceptible to is catfishing. Catfishing scams are ones that an individual pretends to be someone else in order to solicit personal information and/or coerce victims into performing acts against their will. The FBI's Internet Complaint Center has seen a huge increase of this behavior the last few years, reporting it's the number one scam online. With anonymous emails and public images that can easily be stolen, it is not difficult for people to pretend to be someone they are not.

A particular type of catfishing con is a romance scam. Individuals create a fake dating or social network profile and engage in conversation with others. The perpetrator may do this for several reasons: revenge on an ex, financial gain and greed, or loneliness. Romance scams don't just damage bank accounts, but also someone's trust and emotions. It hurts more to be duped and taken advantage of. Many individuals don't report catfishing scams because of feelings of shame and hurt.

Students should be aware of financial scams, in particular catfishing. They should know some warning signs of con artists:

- They give excuses why they can't meet.
- They refuse to use a webcam, Facetime, or Skype.
- Their profiles may only have a few photos and friends.
- They push the relationship quickly and declare their romantic feelings early on.
- They claim to be in the military, or have a job that travels all the time.
- Their stories may be inconsistent and have grammar and spelling errors.

Beyond catfishing there are many other types of financial scams. With the bitcoin rush in 2017, many fraudsters used Instagram to pose with expensive items and tell their followers that they too could be rich if they flip their bitcoin, after an initial investment of course. Multilevel marketing schemes are also popular on social media. These may not be illegal, but it's rare that a person can walk away without losing money. Social media accounts encourage their followers to sign up other members. The US Securities and Exchange Commission cautions that any program that promises high returns in a short time period, doesn't have a clear product, and requires some kind of buy-in with an emphasis on recruiting others is to be avoided.

GPT (Get Paid To) sites are a growing online industry that operate in a gray zone. To get around online gambling laws, some sites do not advertise spending money to get money. These GPT sites say that you can buy "tokens" or that if you complete tasks, you can spin a wheel or get prizes. For example, one GPT product called Piggy Bank claims to pay you in prizes or cash for completing tasks and bringing others to the site. These tasks typically only pay a few cents, the real money comes from recruitment, like a multilevel marketing scheme.

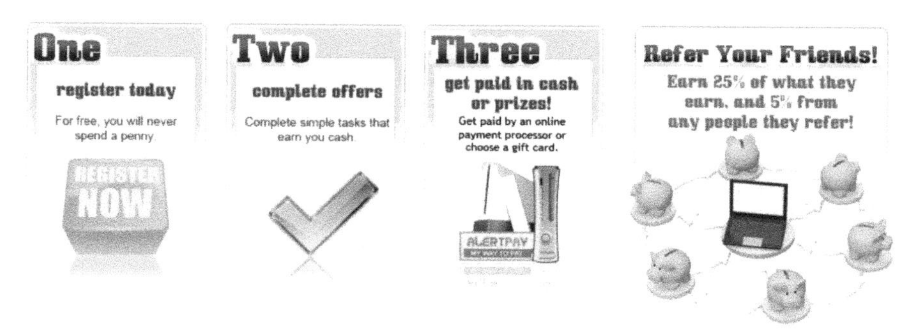

Figure 9.1. Get Paid To website. *Courtesy of the author*

Another gray area and potential scam are loot boxes. These are virtual items in mobile, PC, and console games. They are mystery boxes where you don't know what you're purchasing. Sometimes there is rare content; other times they are useless. Loot boxes are a form of gambling; if you spin a roulette wheel you don't know what you're going to get, you're taking a risk: just like a loot box. The primary audience for these loot boxes is young people, which makes them particularly concerning. Lawmakers in the United States and other countries and video game manufacturers have begun cracking down on loot boxes, calling them gambling, but as of this writing they are legal in most cases and jurisdictions.

Students need to guard their personal and financial data closely. They should never share this information with strangers and should be very suspicious if someone asks for it. Students should know to only buy and sell from people or sites they trust.

They should also be wary of games and sites that make wild promises and should view many online claims with suspicion.

In addition to speaking about the negative issues online, students should know about positive fintech tools. Online marketplaces have made it easier for young people to make money. Teens can sell their art on DeviantArt, share their music on Soundcloud, make money off videos on YouTube, or sell a product on Amazon. There are also budgeting software programs and apps to help young people learn to track their expenditures and plan for the future. The app Mint has an easy-to-use budgeting feature, and there is a teen-friendly mobile payment app currently available called Seqr Go.

SAMPLE DIGITAL COMMERCE ACTIVITY: IS THIS A SCAM?

Materials: Images of potential online financial scams
Instructions:

1. Share with the students that there are a variety of online scams online. Tell them that "catfishing" or "romance" scams are the number one way that people can get conned out of money. Explain that this activity will show them images that they have to identify as a scam or not.
2. Show the images and ask the class if they are scams or not. Have them explain their reasoning. Also, explain that while some scams may be legal, for example loot boxes, they may be unethical.
3. Share with the students questions to ask when identifying online scams:
    a. Where are the posts from? If you don't know, download the image on the poster's profile or what was posted, go to Tools/Settings and "Show Location Info" or do a reverse Google Image search.
    b. Who are the person's followers? Who are the person's top ten friends?
    c. Will the person talk to you? If someone does not want to talk over Facetime or Skype, be suspicious.
    d. How often does the person post? When? Is this individual posting erratically or too much? It may be a bot and not a person. Are the posts in odd hours of the day? The person may be in another time zone and not someone locally.
    e. Is it a verified account? Platforms like Amazon and eBay offer seller reviews and those sellers can be ranked. Facebook, Twitter, and Instagram offer check marks for verified accounts.

Sample discussion questions to encourage self-reflection:

- Why do you think young people might be vulnerable to scams?
- What makes us fall prey to scams?

- Why would "romance" and "catfishing" scams be the number one kind?
- How do you feel if you fall for a scam?

DIGITAL LAW

A 2016 report by the United States Patent and Trademark Office said that nearly 40 percent of the US economy is based on intellectual property (IP). Intellectual property can be everything from algorithms to processes to characters, stories, images, formulas, and more. Intellectual property is big business, and when people don't understand the digital laws protecting IP, they not only hurt other creators, but could also hurt their own creations.

Copyright and Fair Use

Copyright grants exclusive rights to a creator of a work to disseminate, edit, replicate, and manage their creations. These rights are time limited and can be impacted by fair use. Copyright is a form of intellectual property that involves creative works like songs, art, and books. Fair use permits limited use of copyrighted material in nonprofit and educational settings. The use of that copyrighted material has to be less than the whole. This could mean only a few seconds of a song is used, or an image is used but just once in a lesson plan. There are debates on what fair use means in terms of coding, music sampling, and linking to works in news sites.

For example, a decade-long battle over copyright continues between Georgia State University (GSU) and three publishers over fair use of instructional materials. In 2009, three publishers sued Georgia State University for sharing sections of textbooks with students at no charge. The faculty members thought those excerpts constituted fair use. In 2012 a US District court sided against the publishers, but then in 2014 this decision was reversed in the US Court of Appeals. The back-and-forth continued in 2016 as the original 2012 filing was reinstated. But the publishers appealed again in 2017.

As reported in *Inside Higher Ed*, Kevin Smith, dean of libraries at the University of Kansas, commented on the case: "Publishing models have changed. Open access and the movement towards educational resources have had a profound impact on the way course materials are provided to students." Licensing of content has changed the landscape. Fair use can be gotten around if a license is purchased for digital content. The person purchasing the material does not own the content but uses it through that license.

Overseeing those intellectual property laws online is the Digital Millennium Copyright Act (DMCA). It was enacted in 1998 by the United States Congress to bring the United States in alignment with worldwide intellectual property laws. A big impact of the DMCA is that it makes internet service providers exempt from direct and indirect liability. That means that a provider like Comcast cannot be held liable for users who violate copyright laws through their Comcast internet subscription.

There are criticisms of DMCA. Educators in the GSU legal battle felt that fair use should be broader. DMCA limits free use and some say it also limits free expression and hurts the free market by impeding competition. The Electronic Frontier Foundation sued the US government in 2016 for a provision in DMCA but did not win.

How to Teach Digital Law

Educators should bring this debate to their students. Have them understand both sides of the issue. Another issue that students should consider is that we all have electronic responsibilities for behavior online, and that something can be legal but unethical, or ethical but illegal. Here are some question prompts for students:

- What are the positives around copyright? The negatives?
- Do you think people should be able to share what they see online? Why or why not?
- How can limiting what people share and use online be a good thing?
- How can limiting what people share and use online be a negative thing?
- Have you ever run into an issue of copyright before? Has someone ever contacted you about using your work, or you using theirs?

The debate around fair use and copyright continues, and it's an issue that affects young people. Publishers, large tech companies, artists, and others have a strong vested interest to protect their content, and lawsuits and legal issues can result if that is violated.

Students should understand how copyright and intellectual property work online. Some general tips for everyone are:

- **Understand hiring agreements.** If someone else helped you create the content, like a photographer or videographer, you need to make sure you own what they made. This can mean creating a work-for-hire agreement.
- **Read terms of agreements.** Before uploading content online, understand the terms of agreement. Do you still retain ownership once you submit it somewhere?
- **Create your own images.** If you make your own images to use, you do not need to worry about copyright. You can also purchase stock photos, which are copyright free.
- **Link and tag.** Link to the original source of the content and tag groups to attribute content. Also, you may need to send written permission to some content creators to utilize it.
- **Utilize Creative Commons.** Creative Commons is a database with images, music, and more unlicensed content.

- **Assume it's copyrighted.** When online, people just automatically assume that what they see is copyrighted.

The concept of copyright should be introduced to younger students. While elementary students do not need to know all the nuances of copyright, like fair use, they should understand the idea that people's ideas and work should be protected. Below is an activity used with elementary students to introduce that concept.

SAMPLE COPYRIGHT ACTIVITY: PAPER SELFIES

Materials: Sheet of paper for each student, pencils or other writing utensils
Instructions:

1. Give each student a blank sheet of paper and writing utensil.
2. Give them two to three minutes to draw a picture of themselves, a paper selfie.
3. Discuss.
4. Optional: Have the students give their paper selfie to a partner and have that partner scribble on it. During the discussion ask them how it felt when that happened.

Sample discussion questions for Copyright Activity

- How would you feel if someone tried to take your paper selfie without asking permission?
- How would you feel if someone scribbled over your paper selfie?
- What happens when we bully someone online? Can that be erased?

DIGITAL RIGHTS AND RESPONSIBILITIES

I was teaching in a class of high school students about what you can and can't say online. One student was upset by what I said and told me indignantly, "It's the Internet, you can say whatever you want. If people choose to get upset with it that's their problem." This student, like all the others, had been raised with a story that the Internet is a free, wild-west, democratic place where people could do as they please. But it's not. There are public forums and private forums. There are fences and firewalls. Many do not understand this concept, and their digital rights and responsibilities.

—Story from the author

What are your rights online? What are your responsibilities? That is a complicated question that may depend on where you live, who you are, and what platform you're on. There are no simple black-and-white answers, and the belief that you can do *anything* online is false.

Digital rights and responsibilities entail having the right and freedom to use all types of digital technology while using the technology in an acceptable and appropriate manner. Those who use the internet have a right to privacy and personal expression, within limits.

When US citizens think of freedom of speech they may think of the Bill of Rights and the First Amendment. The First Amendment states, "Congress shall make no law respecting an establishment of religion, or prohibiting the free exercise thereof; or abridging the freedom of speech, or of the press; or the right of the people peaceably to assemble, and to petition the government for a redress of grievances."

The First Amendment was created long before the internet, and the rights enshrined there continue to be hotly debated. The founders surely did not predict that one day in the future there would be an interlinking global forum called the internet. Applying the words of an eighteenth-century document to modern-day online activity is difficult and not always relevant. Despite that, the belief that since individuals have a right to "freedom of speech" they can say whatever they want online has existed since the internet began.

Yes, the internet gives you rights, but there are responsibilities that accompany those rights. An example of this can be seen with defamation and libel laws. In the United States, United Kingdom, Canada, and other countries, defamation and libel are considered a civil wrong and can be prosecuted. Libel refers to making false public assertions that hurt another person. Slander is the spoken communication of false assertions that cause damage.

Defamation lawsuits are difficult to prove and win in the United States, but they still happen. In 2018, Alex Jones, who runs the controversial talk show *InfoWars* was sued by the parents of a victim from the Sandy Hook massacre. In 2012, twenty-year old Adam Lanza shot and killed twenty children and six adult staff members at the Sandy Hook Elementary School before killing himself and his mother. Alex Jones has made statements on Twitter, on his show, and other mediums claiming that the shootings were a staged hoax. He claimed on *InfoWars* that no one was murdered at Sandy Hook Elementary and is reported as saying in 2014, "I've looked at it and undoubtedly there's a cover-up, there's actors, they're manipulating, they've been caught lying, and they were pre-planning before it and rolled out with it." Jones's lawyers tried to dismiss the lawsuit, but as of fall 2018 it is progressing forward; in addition, *InfoWars* has been banned from social media channels like YouTube, Apple podcasts, and Facebook.

Jones is an egregious example, but his situation demonstrates that people cannot just say whatever they want online. There are restrictions. Beyond libel and slander, other areas of restricted free speech are:

- **Words or actions meant to incite violence or influence others to commit violence.** An example of pushback to this is the alt-right using the platform Discord to engage in hate speech and plan the Charlottesville Unite the Right Rally. Users were banned from Discord in August 2017 after the rally.

- **Child pornography.** Storing, disseminating, and sharing child pornography is illegal.
- **Speech in a private forum.** Private organizations like schools, businesses, and others can make their own policies around free speech.

There is confusion on public and private forums online. Not all online spaces are public. Users sign agreements to use platforms like YouTube, Discord, and Facebook. Those user agreements can limit usage and free speech. They can do that because they are not public spaces. Christopher Gates of the Sunlight Foundation writes, "Our shared conversations are increasingly taking place in a privately owned and managed walled gardens."

Should there be an internet Bill of Rights? This can be a good question for an educator to pose to their students. Some people, most notably Tim Berners-Lee, who is often credited as being the creator of the World Wide Web, says we need one. On the twenty-fifth anniversary of the internet in 2014, Berners-Lee expressed his hope saying, "I ask you to join in—to help us imagine and build the future standards for the web, and to press for every country to develop a digital bill of rights to advance a free and open web for everyone."

What does freedom mean to people? What is a right? Those are big questions that would need to have some consensus for an internet Bill of Rights. What's problematic about determining freedom and rights is that those answers depend on a cultural and sociological perspective. A "right" to an American may be very different to someone in China. The internet originally came from the United States, and US-centric beliefs have been spread through its channels. However, should the United States be telling other countries how to believe? And even if someone from a country other than the United States believed in a free and open internet, it does not mean anything if their local laws deny or abuse rights.

Young people should understand and talk about these issues. They need to know their rights in order to protect and advocate for them. By knowing their rights, they can also advocate and support others. Young people should understand that rights are not a given, not unchangeable or unalienable; they differ with governments, institutions, and beliefs.

Here are some discussion questions for educators to guide conversations around digital rights and responsibilities:

- What are your digital rights?
- What are your responsibilities?
- Are there times when someone's right might hurt someone else? If that occurs, what do you think should happen?
- Who should determine what people's online rights and responsibilities are?
- Should there be an internet Bill of Rights? If so, what should it say?
- Is it fair that private companies can limit free speech? Why or why not?
- What type of free speech should be limited? Why?

Online Privacy

Online privacy is a concept that relates to several elements of digital citizenship. Understanding online privacy is important for digital safety and security. It also relates to digital health and wellness because privacy that's violated or requirements to share too much information can affect emotional health. The concept of privacy in digital communication pertains to knowing what to share and when to stay silent. Privacy also relates to digital literacy, understanding terms of agreements, how to change settings, and how to block or restrict apps or individuals.

Online privacy is described here as part of digital rights and responsibilities because an individual has a right to privacy. This is a controversial subject that is debated more in the media, in front of lawmakers, and among users. People who may not have considered online privacy before might now be thinking about it because of all the attention it has received.

What do students think about online privacy? From our work teaching this concept to K–12 students the answer is "Not much."

I surveyed a middle school class about passwords and other privacy concepts. How many passwords did they have? Did they know their passwords? Did they change their passwords? Who else had access to their device?

A few students looked confused. The concept of changing passwords was foreign to them. They didn't understand some of the questions.

Most of the students in that class had one password across all their logins. Some of them did not know that master password, it was just automatically saved on their device. The passwords they used were simple and easy to guess. One student commented that she didn't see a need for passwords because of her thumbprint login. Several of them regularly shared their devices with friends, and didn't see an issue with that because they trusted them.

Pew Research, as part of their Internet and American Life Project in 2012–2013, surveyed adolescents about their online privacy habits and found similar findings. They reported that 60 percent of teens said that they are "not too" concerned or "not at all" concerned about others having access to their data. Only 9 percent said they are "very" concerned. These statistics may have changed since that survey due to high-profile data breaches and the controversies with Facebook and Cambridge Analytica. However, in our experience, teens do not think very much about privacy online.

What does this mean for adults who work with teens? Don't make assumptions. Don't shame or tell them that they're wrong. These teens have grown up in a different environment where the internet has always existed, so they may have never thought about these ideas.

A galvanizing force behind the recent conversations around online privacy is Facebook. The company has faced push-back and investigations on their role in spreading fake news and divisive content during the 2016 US presidential election. In spring of 2018, news about the Cambridge Analytica scandal came out. It was found that millions of users' Facebook data was shared with the political firm without their knowledge and that data was used to create divisive ads and posts.

In summer of 2018, it was found that Facebook had data-sharing agreements with apps and foreign countries that allowed access to user data. In fall of 2018, more security issues arose and Facebook was investigated by the FBI for the exposure of personal information of over thirty million users. Another security issue was found near the end of 2018 that may have exposed photos of over six million users. Facebook is currently under investigation and there will most likely be other online privacy concerns exposed.

Online privacy scandals did not just happen to Facebook in 2018; they also occurred with Uber, Google, and Amazon. It leaves one wondering if we can expect *any* online privacy?

What right to privacy does an individual have? What type of data should companies be allowed to collect? Should governments be involved in online privacy discussions? These are questions that are being asked by more and more individuals, and young people should consider them too.

Educators cannot control what large tech companies or governments decide to do, but they can help their students understand online privacy. Understanding privacy regulations and making steps to protect oneself is a protective factor against potential negative online consequences like data breaches, scams, and more.

SAMPLE ONLINE PRIVACY ACTIVITY

See appendix F for the Creating Safe Passwords worksheet.
Materials: Creating Safe Passwords worksheet, pen or pencil
Instructions:

1. Explain to the group about how others would like your personal data for various reasons. Passwords can help protect personal data. Ask the class where you would use a strong password.
2. Pass out Creating Safe Passwords worksheet.
3. Talk about the different ways of creating a strong password:
   - A passphrase is an easy to remember password that is harder to crack.
   - A passphrase is composed of letters, symbols, abbreviations, and numbers.
4. Discuss the importance of passwords and how they can use their new password to keep their data safe.

Sample discussion questions for Creating Safe Passwords Activity:

- What types of websites do you think need the strongest passwords? Why?
- Why do you think it may not be the best idea to have the same password for every website?
- Why is it important to have a password you can remember?
- What are some other options for security beyond passwords? (i.e., thumbprint, facial recognition, etc.)

Resources for Online Privacy

There are organizations that work for a free and open internet and more privacy from institutions. They regularly report on what's going on in the global world of online privacy, offer resources to protect yourself, and some even have suggestions for young people to learn more.

- **Electronic Frontier Foundation (EFF):** The EFF is an international nonprofit based in San Francisco that advocates for digital privacy as well as provides resources and tools.
- **American Library Association (ALA):** The ALA regularly publishes and advocates on the topic of online privacy and has published a Library Bill of Rights which includes privacy.
- **Library Freedom Project:** The Library Freedom Project helps librarians and other educators protect the privacy of their patrons and students. They offer advice and privacy toolkits for adults and children.
- **Mozilla Foundation:** This nonprofit which supports the Firefox browser and other software offers support and advice related to online privacy.
- **Tor:** Tor is a free software that helps protect online privacy. Their website has resources and information about how to protect oneself against surveillance.

10

Making Digital Citizenship Inclusive

One lesson that really stuck with the students at the detention center was about digital footprint, recalled instructor Spring Lavallee. She was teaching an eight-week digital citizenship class to students in custody. Spring was talking to the students about how what you post online can be found and seen by others. During that lesson the stories came in. One student cited Facebook as the reason he was arrested. The police had seen things he had posted and brought him in. The digital footprint can affect individuals in positive ways or, unfortunately in this instance, negative ways. Another lesson later in the series focused on how to work to push down the negative news online, by creating positive content. Hopefully, these students' digital footprint will not follow them the rest of their lives.

—Story from the author

Educators know that students are not one-size-fits-all creatures. What's important to one student may not be relevant to another. What one student has known since preschool may be new information to another. For the students in detention, the concept of a digital footprint was very important, although that instruction came too late for some. Every student is unique; thus, teaching digital citizenship must be adapted to the needs of students. This chapter will explore risk factors with certain populations, research, and strategies for educators to more inclusively teach digital citizenship.

In fall of 2018 Digital Respons-Ability taught eight digital citizenship classes to students at a juvenile detention center. The students, while somewhat skeptical at first, having never heard of digital citizenship, warmed up to the teacher and the curriculum. They posted gains in knowledge but taught us more.

Our curriculum is being adapted to put more focus on digital communication, digital literacy, and understanding digital footprint. These were the areas that were most relevant to these students in their current situation: a liminal space where they are contained before they get back to home and school. We look forward to more work with students in state care and custody in 2019.

WHAT ASSUMPTIONS DO WE MAKE WHEN TEACHING DIGITAL CITIZENSHIP?

We all make assumptions. Forming assumptions and generalizations helps us process the terabytes of information our world constantly throws at us. With a class of twenty, thirty, or even forty students, we have to make certain assumptions to transmit any kind of information in a short time period.

For example, we may assume the entire class speaks English or writes on grade level. Assumptions are not inherently bad, but they can impede learning. Each subject has its own assumptions; to teach algebra you assume one knows how to multiply; a computer science instructor may assume the class knows how to type. Teaching digital citizenship typically involves assumptions, and this section will seek to debunk them.

Digital Access

Digital access, a foundational element of digital citizenship, comes loaded with assumptions. Access is not created equal. Consider the example of two students who technically have digital access. One is in an area that has fiber optic connections. She can reach the internet quickly at home, school, and across multiple devices. Her caregivers pay low fees for that access, and she can trust that it will always be there. Another student lives in a more rural area of the state and relies on satellite access. He cannot be sure that he can get on the internet at home, and it is many miles away to any other internet access point. He has to rely on his cell phone's data plan when the speed is particularly slow or intermittent.

Technically both students are connected. They have devices to connect to the internet, they know how to connect online, but one has reliable and high-speed broadband, while the other does not. The student who cannot rely on the internet may get behind in online homework or not be able to stream certain videos required in class.

In 2018, Pew Research reported almost a fifth of students do not have a high-speed connection at home and struggle to finish their homework. Over time, the student with better access becomes more digitally literate and a more engaged digital citizen.

Most students will have digital access. The Federal Communications Commission has issued a Broadband Deployment report since the 1990s. In 2018 it reported that as of the end of 2016, 92.3 percent of Americans had broadband access of speeds of 25 Mbps. While that's a good thing, and it's a percentage that has risen in recent years, it only paints part of the picture. That speed is a basic requirement for actions like viewing a webpage, downloading a song, or watching a short video. However, things start slowing down with longer movies, streaming TV, or high-definition (HD) videos. At 25 Mbps, it would take an hour to download an HD movie.

Compare that speed to fiber connections, which can reach up to 500 Mbps. But that access is more limited and scattershot across the United States. Broadband Now estimates only about 25 percent of the United States has fiber coverage. And that percentage can vary widely depending on what state you live in. For example, Rhode Island has the most fiber coverage at 85 percent according to Broadband Now, but the nearby state of Connecticut only has about 3 percent of the population covered.

That gap in access is referred to as the digital divide. There is a well reported digital access divide between rural and urban, Caucasian and other races, and higher and lower incomes. According to the FCC, over 15 million Americans in rural and tribal areas lack broadband at speeds of 10 Mbps. Individuals in low-income households do not have the same access, and this is particularly felt by the children of those homes. Pew Research reports that a third of households with children making under $30,000 do not have a high-speed connection. One group of students affected the most by the digital divide are African Americans. About a quarter of black adolescents report to Pew Research that they sometimes can't finish their homework at home; only 4 percent of Caucasian students said the same thing.

Lack of internet access can exacerbate existing societal, class, and racial disparities. Well-meaning teachers, trying to encourage online research and digital literacy skills, may be inadvertently creating hardships at home. This is a tough situation, because students need those skills and teachers have no control over what type of digital access their class has at home. Not making assumptions can help. Instructors can also evaluate their class requirements. Many lessons can be taught without internet access. Are we using the internet for homework because it's better or because we have to? Or are we using the internet because it's easier?

Other questions instructors should consider:

- How much of my assignments require internet access?
- How do I allow my students to submit assignments? Can they only turn them in online?
- How much streaming online video content do I require my students to watch? Can they be allowed to watch those videos in school?

Digital Literacy

Digital inclusion is digital literacy along with digital access and the hardware to access the internet. To be fully digitally inclusive, an individual must have internet access, the hardware such as a phone or computer to get online, and the skills to know how to connect and navigate the web. Digital citizens are digitally inclusive.

Imagine you have received a device from an alien species. This slate-colored box is supposed to have answers to all the questions in the universe. You have it in your hand, and you know what it's supposed to do, but you have no idea how to use it. You are familiar with the slate-colored boxes on Earth that can give you answers at an instant, but this new box has unfamiliar symbols, and you can't seem to find the "on" switch. While this box may be a valuable artifact, it is as useless as a slate-colored rock if you can't use it. The knowledge of *how* to use something, can be more valuable than the thing itself.

Digital literacy deciphers the alien-like symbols, characters, memes, and words across technology. It instructs on what buttons to press, how to handle technology, how to type, how to adapt technology and change its settings, and much more. And digital literacy, like digital access, comes with its own assumptions.

Through 2016–2017 I taught several cohorts of refugees how to use a computer. It was a six-month federally funded program through Salt Lake Community College. We worked intensively with a class of adults for six months, with individuals who may have never touched a computer before in their lives. Some of my students were very new to the United States and had been in refugee camps for years. When they arrived in the country, they were continually asked to fill out forms online to apply for jobs and services, connect with family, and more. These students proactively took time out of their busy schedules for several classes a week over a six-month period. They knew that using a computer was vital for success in their new country, but it was not an easy process.

I remember teaching the very basics of what a computer is at the beginning of a new six-month cohort. I explained what a monitor was, a keyboard, and a mouse. I walked them through turning on and off a computer and how to use a mouse. While teaching them with the mouse I told them to "click here" and "click there" and while doing so heard a sound coming from a student. He was doing exactly what I said, he was clicking here and there, but with his mouth.

He had never used a mouse before and did not know what "click" meant. And why would he? He was new to English, the United States, and computers. A mouse was an alien object to him, but he had a teacher who was explaining things, and he was trying to learn.

I learned through my experience teaching refugees that I had to throw most of my assumptions out the window. To them a "window" meant something that showed you the outside, and a "click" meant a verbal noise. Understanding that not everyone shares the same vocabulary is an important part of a digitally inclusive classroom.

When teaching digital literacy, we must take special care to explain vocabulary first. A student, particularly an adolescent, will probably not want to ask a question and seem ignorant. So, if no one asks you to explain a term, it might not mean they all really understand it. Explaining vocabulary terms will not only help you teach, but it will help your students understand. Have them explain what concepts like "settings" or "typing" mean.

Also, consider that some students, like those from other cultures or countries, may have special strengths with digital literacy. These students may be the only ones who understand technology in their home. They also might be the main English speakers in a family still learning the language. These students must be able to explain complicated technology subjects in both English and another language. Consider letting these bilingual students teach their peers.

There is a popular subreddit called Explain Like I'm Five, or ELI5, where users post questions like "Why is space black" or "Why are some allergies more common?" Then other users respond to those questions using very simple but elaborate language. It's not easy to do. To really break down a topic and explain it to an imaginary five-year-old takes a deep understanding of the topic. Have your students explain step-by-step how they made that video, or what a popular meme actually means. It will challenge them and make them think.

Digital Communication

While usage of the largest social media platforms like Facebook, YouTube, Instagram, Snapchat, and Twitter is fairly constant, there are divides. For example, Latinos use the messaging service WhatsApp more than other communication platforms. Black and Hispanic individuals are more likely to use Facebook and Instagram than whites, but not by a high percentage.

Outside of the United States, racial and cultural divides affect social media use even more. According to the nonprofit Freedom House's *Freedom on the Net 2018* report, China is the most digitally authoritarian country in the world. China bans popular social media sites like Facebook, YouTube, and others in favor of the government-influenced WeChat. Other social media platforms like LINE, Viber, or Weibo have more popularity outside of the United States. Some, like TikTok, formerly Musical.ly, started in another country and came to the United States.

Household income levels influence social media use. Pinterest, LinkedIn, Instagram, and Twitter are all used by those with higher income levels of $75,000+ than households making less than $30,000 a year. Gaps in educational attainment can influence this. The usage of LinkedIn is, understandably, higher in college graduates, with Pew Research reporting that just 9 percent of individuals with a high school diploma or less use it.

Social media use is another assumption that educators should be wary of making. Understanding that not *everyone* uses Facebook or *everyone* knows what LinkedIn is can help students feel more included.

Emoji, often trivialized by adults, are a universal language. We understand images. Images on cave walls were our human ancestors' first language. This was discovered firsthand by working with refugee children. These children spoke a variety of languages: Arabic, Kirundi, French, Swahili, and others. Some were fluent in English, others not. But they could understand emoji.

In several activities the children were asked to participate in polls and other discussions through emoji. They would hold up a thumbs up sign, or a heart, or a smiley face. The students were also asked to tell their family story through emoji. After drawing on a worksheet, some students came up to the front and told their story through emoji and other symbols. Emoji provided a means for students to communicate across language.

Figure 10.1. Refugee student participating in an emoji activity. *Courtesy of the author*

An assumption an educator may make is that all students are fluent in English. Fluency can range dramatically, even with native born populations. A student that struggles with language will most likely find concepts like digital etiquette difficult. To be able to properly respond and communicate online, one must be familiar with written language.

In addition, students from other countries, like the refugee children, may find slang terms, idioms, and acronyms particularly confusing. Slang is widely used across digital platforms and beyond. Common cyberspeak like LOL (laughing out loud), or BTW (by the way) have even found their way into regular and sometimes formal written communication. Think about having a vocabulary lesson that includes slang and text speak—perhaps the adult in the room will learn something too.

For a worksheet to create emoji stories, see appendix G.

POTENTIAL GAINS FROM WORKING WITH SPECIAL POPULATIONS

Educators can make a strong impact by teaching digital citizenship to special populations. These are groups that may have never been taught these skills at home and at school. Also, institutional and other challenges prevent the teaching of digital citizenship. Some schools and organizations may have more resources to offer this type of curriculum such as having qualified media specialists, computer labs, smaller class sizes, and support of administrators.

Since digital citizenship is a multidisciplinary subject with elements spread across subjects, it takes a dedicated push for those lessons to be taught. Young people with special needs may have more of their class day with speech pathologists and physical therapists, allowing less time for digital citizenship. Students in custody have little to no access to the internet, making digital citizenship a lower priority. Children in overcrowded classrooms with busy teachers, may find this type of learning pushed aside for logistical issues. Students who struggle with language may have their days filled with extra classes and may just be trying to keep up.

The teaching of digital citizenship is not equitable, and unfortunately those young people who do not have the same advantages may be missing out. This is a loss because there is research to suggest that these are the students who need it the most. The small cohort at the juvenile detention facility referenced at the beginning of this chapter had larger gains than another adolescent digital citizenship class taught a month earlier. Another impact with that population was increasing interest in STEM-related careers. For students in poverty, like most that are incarcerated, STEM fields can be a higher-paying path for long-term success.

In summer 2018, Digital Respons-Ability launched a research study with Utah State University on teaching digital citizenship to two cohorts of refugee students in grades Kindergarten through sixth grade. The cohorts of students were divided by age and taught the same six-class program with a few adaptations due to age. Data from the quantitative survey questions given to the older cohort in grades four to six were compared to non-refugee students of a similar class size in the summer of 2017. Both sets of students came from Title 1 schools, but for one cohort the majority were native born while the refugee group had mostly students from outside the United States.

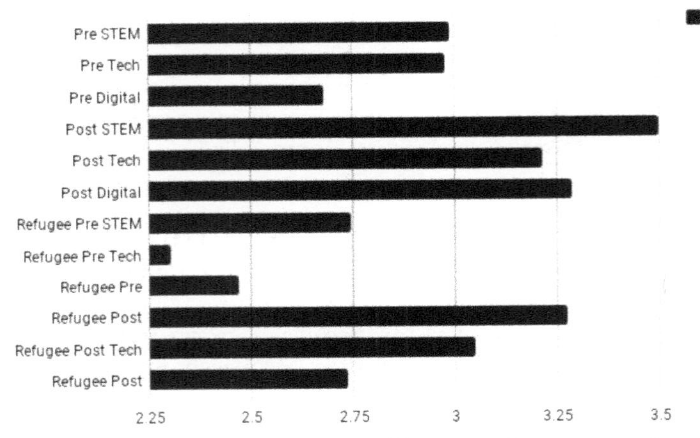

Figure 10.2. Refugee digital citizenship survey data vs. non-refugee digital citizenship survey data. ***Courtesy of the author***

When comparing pre- and post-class scores, the refugee students came to class with less interest and knowledge. Thus, they reported larger increase in scores. This is an opportunity for educators.

Other findings from the research study with refugee students include:

- Students born in the United States have higher levels of interest in technology and STEM. This may be due to more exposure to the topics.

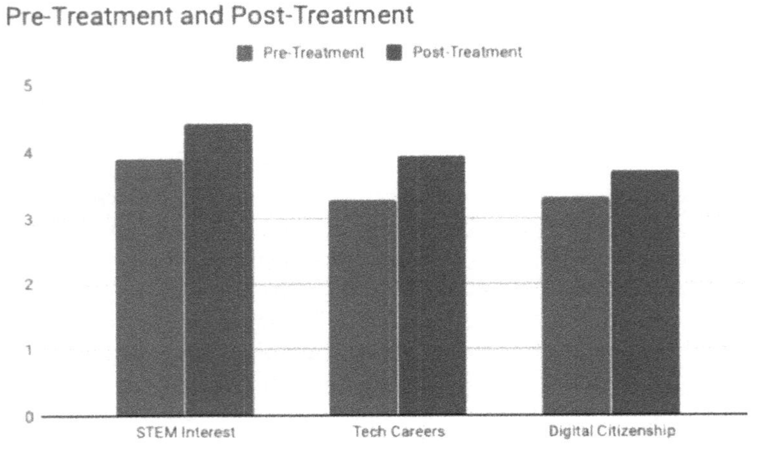

Figure 10.3. Graph of results from digital citizenship class with students in custody. ***Courtesy of the author***

- Students born in the United States have higher levels of interest and knowledge in digital citizenship.
- Students born outside of the United States struggle more with English and have less technical vocabulary as it relates to digital citizenship.

Educators will need to work on pushing aside their assumptions, but if they can do that, teaching digital citizenship to students with unique needs has the potential for making significant changes in knowledge and interests.

PREVENTION SCIENCE AND DIGITAL CITIZENSHIP WITH SPECIAL POPULATIONS

Prevention science asks practitioners to focus on groups and individuals with certain risk factors that make them more likely to engage in delinquent behaviors or be a victim of violence or abuse. By focusing on smaller groups or single individuals, resources and funding can be distributed in the most efficient way. Not everyone starts off on the same level playing field. We are not blank slates, and our individual genes and life experiences create risk factors that societies and individuals must work to overcome.

Dr. Diana Fishbein, a neuroscientist and the director of the National Prevention Science Coalition (https://www.npscoalition.org), advocates for prevention science at the national level. "If we can prevent the problems early, we don't have to worry about what happens when they become entrenched in the individual or in the fabric of society or in a family. We are disrupting the process that may lead to negative outcomes." Despite that uneven playing field, prevention science holds out hope.

One area of new research is epigenetics. Dr. Fishbein holds out much hope for epigenetics, which is the study of inherited changes in gene function.

> Our environment has an impact on the way genes function. The exciting part for prevention science is that even after there's damage through the epigenome through trauma it's reversible. . . . There's so much potential to show how we can improve developmental trajectories that have been traumatized or have experienced poverty and caregiver addiction, the whole host of adversities that can alter childhood development negatively. The damage can be seen in the epigenome, and the reversal of that damage has the potential to improve those pathways.

A selection of risk factors for certain populations are highlighted in table 10.1 based on research from the Centers for Disease Control and Prevention.

There are more risk factors that could be listed and attached to other behaviors like substance abuse and sexual violence. However, this chart was not made to provide an exhaustive list but point out that individuals with unique needs and barriers are at high risk.

In addition, many individuals with mental health concerns and disabilities have comorbidity: multiple diseases and disorders. For example, those with autism spec-

Table 10.1. Risk Factors for Youth Violence and Suicide

	Mental Health	*Disability*	*Poverty*
Risk Factor for Youth Violence	Attention deficits, hyperactivity or learning disorders	Low IQ	Diminished economic activities
Risk Factor for Youth Violence	Poor behavioral control	Lack of involvement in conventional activities	Low parental education and income
Risk Factor for Suicide	History of mental disorders, particularly clinical depression	Physical illness	Barriers to accessing mental health treatment
Risk Factor for Suicide	Feelings of hopelessness	Isolation, a feeling of being cut off from other people	Loss (relational, social, work, or financial)

trum disorder (ASD) have a high comorbidity rate, reported to be anywhere from 11 to 84 percent for anxiety disorders. A person living in poverty is also more likely to have comorbidity with attention-deficit/hyperactivity disorder (ADHD), ASD, and asthma. Poverty is a risk factor for those conditions according to a 2017 study published in the journal *Pediatrics*.

For a person in poverty or who has a mental illness or disability, the playing field is not only not level, it's strewn with rocks. These individuals are most likely dealing with multiple risk factors and disorders. Thus, a caregiver or educator needs to look at the whole person and keep in mind multiple concerns.

Teaching Digital Citizenship to Individuals with Disabilities or Mental Illness

It is difficult to generalize when providing teaching recommendations for individuals with disabilities or mental illness. Each person is unique, and their concerns may manifest in a different way. For example, there's a saying in the autism community, "If you've met one person with autism, you've met one person with autism." Someone with autism may engage in some of the stereotypical behaviors like stimming or flapping of the hands, but others may have no such behaviors. The same axiom can also be applied to those with mental illnesses like depression. Extroverted and apparently "happy" people can be severely depressed. Despite the difficulty, I will share a few tips from my experience teaching digital citizenship to students who fall in these categories.

Provide More Movement Activities

Individuals with ADHD or ASD need to move around. When teaching afterschool, this is even more important. A student with autism may have had to put on a mask and try to be social and sit all day. That student may be bursting to let that mask down after school. Allow the opportunity for that.

Movement activities may be simple. For example, when having a discussion on a digital citizenship–related topic, divide the room in two. Ask a simple question like, "Do you like social media?" Instead of the students raising their hands or verbalizing, they go to one side of the room. Go through a list of these questions and have students cross the room to one side or another based on their response.

Include Sensory and Fidget Items

The excess energy that may come from individuals who have kept it in all day, needs to have an outlet. In addition to movement activities, provide something they can do with their hands. This can be a coloring page, puzzle, squishy materials, and so on.

For a digital citizenship coloring page that can be copied and used in class see appendix H.

Talk Less, Show More

Individuals with disabilities may struggle to understand speech. This can be because of hearing disabilities or how their brain works. For example, individuals with autism can struggle to understand non-literal sayings like slang and idioms. Provide more pictures and images to illustrate your point.

Understand That Technology Has Different Effects on People

Technology can be a positive or negative for individuals with sensory processing or attention disorders. The blinking lights, sounds, and constant novelty make it hard for some to engage with or put away a device. For those who are suffering from anxiety or depression, social media can make it worse.

A 2018 Common Sense Media national survey of adolescents found that, overall, teens found that social media had a positive impact. However, teens who already reported feelings of depression were more likely to find a negative impact. The 10 percent of teens in the survey who said they "are often sad and depressed and aren't very happy with their lives," had about 20 percent increase in negative feelings because of social media.

When working with individuals with mental illness, emphasize positive things to do online. This could be things like:

- commenting positively on others' posts
- planning an event with a friend

- collaborating on a project
- creating art, music, or writing

For students who are dealing with ADHD or ASD, pay particular emphasis to digital health. Help them proactively make goals to limit their tech use and think about why they are using it.

SAMPLE ACTIVITY FOR INDIVIDUALS WITH SPECIAL NEEDS: SENSORY WALK

Materials: None
Instructions:
The sensory walk is a meditation and activity that can be completed anywhere. The goal of the walk is to increase mindfulness, body awareness, and sensory processing. Ideally it is done outside but can also be done inside.

1. The instructor leads students on a preplanned outdoor sensory walk that includes three to five focus points. At the beginning of the walk ask students: "How does your body feel right now?"
2. At the first focus point have the students touch the objects, close their eyes, and listen to the sounds around them and/or smell objects close by. After a few minutes, move to the next focus point.
3. After several focus points, return to the class to continue the lesson.

Teaching Digital Citizenship to Lower-Income Individuals

When teaching digital citizenship, remember that access is not universal. Those who come from circumstances of poverty or lower income are more likely not to have high-speed broadband access, a computer at home, or adult caregivers with the digital literacy skills to help or teach them. Assuming all these students have the same access, know the same software or hardware, or have the digital skills can inadvertently create guilt or shame. Students want to fit in with their peers; highlighting differences they may have with their peers instead of similarities can create a less inclusive atmosphere.

Spend additional time with digital literacy concepts and terms. Instead of saying "open up this file," show where the file is and the steps to find it. Instead of saying, "Download that PowerPoint," explain what exactly a PowerPoint is.

Teaching Digital Citizenship to Students Who Are Refugees or Immigrants

Approximately one-fourth of students in United States public schools are from a refugee or immigrant background according to a 2016 article in *Educational Studies*.

Any instructor across the country is most likely going to have at least one immigrant student in class. As noted earlier, teaching digital citizenship to these students can have a big impact.

From our research in summer of 2018 we found some tips and strategies for teaching digital citizenship to students from other cultures and countries:

- Include movement activities and games. One of the most engaging activities in the group of refugee elementary students involved dressing up with props and acting out online scenes.
- Most likely, refugee and immigrant students have little to no exposure to digital citizenship. Spend extra time on vocabulary.
- Refugees are at higher risk of mental health issues and the effects of trauma. There may be more classroom disruptions than normal; work to mitigate this with frequent breaks, activities, and additional staff if possible.
- Incorporate social and emotional learning skills such as conflict resolution and critical thinking, and encourage peer-to peer communication in small groups.

There are other special populations not covered in this chapter, such as homeless youth and LGBTQ+. They have their unique needs and risk factors as well. It is not easy to make an inclusive classroom and address those risk factors, but you don't need a special degree to do it. Dr. Fishbein said, "Prevention science is an inherently multidisciplinary science. It includes behavioral sciences and more. There are very few people who have a degree in prevention science, they come from a number of different disciplines but have come together to apply prevention science."

Instructors most likely have practices and strategies they are doing already to make their students feel included. For example, mindfulness and meditation are protective practices that can be used across cultures and risk factors. It can be difficult to make behavioral change, particularly as an educator who is working to balance the needs of one student versus a whole classroom. But it's possible. Understanding prevention science and the risk and protective factors can help.

Conclusion

Students are spending an increasing amount of time in front of a screen. This is neither good or bad, it's just the reality of living in our connected twenty-first-century world. Educators and administrators can wring their hands and craft policies based on nostalgia and anxiety or confront the situation that technology is here to stay. By viewing the internet and electronic devices as an opportunity, not an obstacle, educators can make an impactful difference on young people's lives. These students will grow up to use the internet to find a college, determine their career, date, and perhaps later use it to find advice on how to guide their own children with whatever tech there is twenty years from now.

Technology will continue to evolve; by the time this book is in print some tech forecasts will be fulfilled or looked at as laughable by readers. However, humans evolve much more slowly. Our brains are basically the same structure they were thousands of years ago. That's why we must educate and make policy decisions around the much more advanced microprocessor in the brain, not the one in a phone. We must look deeply at the "whys" of behavior and not be distracted by shiny objects that influence but do not cause the behavior.

If you want to make long-lasting change in your classroom or organization, you must look at these questions and the whole person. Digital citizenship is not simply online safety, it's the examination of motivations, biases, patterns, and desires. When we teach digital literacy, we do not simply teach "press here"; we work to understand the other person so that what we're saying makes sense within their context. When we teach online safety, it's not effective to say, "don't cyberbully." We must try to grasp what leads individuals to cyberbully and replace those motivations with something else. When we teach digital commerce it's not enough to say, "this is what a scam looks like." We must understand the reasons people fall for scams, such as the desire for affection. People are complicated. But digital citizenship does not have to be.

Educators can make a digital change in their organization tomorrow. By simply changing a mind-set on technology, the foundation is created. Most activities described in this book do not need many, if any, materials. You do not need to have a degree in computer science to effectively teach digital literacy skills. And you don't need to be a lawyer to instruct on digital law.

Digital citizenship is not typically taught in schools; it's still a new and growing practice. Students may not have any instruction on this subject, at home or school. This is another opportunity for educators to make a difference. You can be that person who looks at the "whys" and connects with a young person. You can create digital citizens.

Appendix A

Digital Citizenship Gap Analysis

Category	*Current State*	*Desired State*	*Action*	*Priority*	*Ownership*
Respect: Access, Etiquette, Law					
Educate: Communication, Literacy, Commerce					
Protect: Rights and Responsibilities, Health and Wellness, Safety and Security					

Appendix B

Robot Maze Activity

Preparation: Before the class begins, create the large six-foot-square Robot Maze using masking tape and a yard stick. Write all of the vocabulary words on the whiteboard.

Materials:

- Masking Tape
- Yard Stick
- Whiteboard, Markers, and Eraser

Technical Vocabulary:

- Coding—The language computers use to communicate.
- Program—(v.) The act of writing code for a computer.
- Command—Each individual instructional step given to a computer.
- Algorithm—A set of commands needed to complete a specific action.
- Looping—Repeating a command or algorithm a set number of times.
- Bug—A mistake in the command or algorithm.

Goal: Students will become familiar with the technical vocabulary and begin to use it in appropriate contexts. Students will understand the basics of computational thinking and how computer coding works. As a group, students will complete their first coding project and write their first algorithm.

Activity: Computer coding is the language we use to speak to computers and tell them what to do. Today we are going to learn how to code by guiding a human robot through our maze. First, we'll need a volunteer robot.

(5 minutes) Demonstrate that the robot can only move when given very specific instructions on how to move/where to go. For example, if the robot is told to move forward one step, it should only take that one step forward; no additional steps should be taken, the robot should not turn its body. What happens if we give the wrong directions or incomplete directions to the robot? We need to be specific and direct in our instructions. Let's help this robot move through the maze by giving it instructions with our words.

(5 minutes) Now that we have shown the robot how to move through the maze, we are going to start writing down the instructions we need to help the robot complete the maze. Every step or turn in our instructions is called a command. When we finish the whole maze, that list of commands is called an algorithm. Let's write our first command on the board. How should the robot move first? (Guide the students through the rest of this activity, writing down directional commands on the whiteboard so they can see what coding looks like.)

(5 minutes) Let's look at our algorithm. Does anyone see any mistakes, maybe where the commands don't match up with what the robot is supposed to do? Those mistakes are called bugs, and sometimes they can mess up the way we want our robot

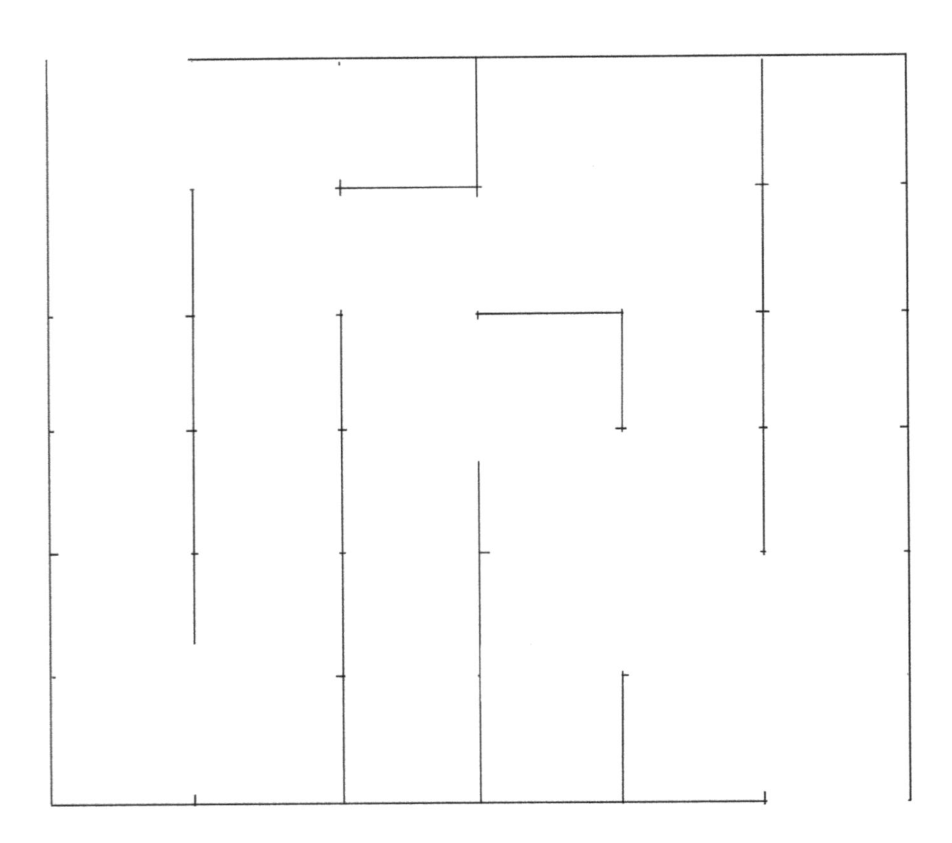

or computer to work. Does anyone else notice something about our algorithm? It looks like there is a pattern of steps right here, where the robot goes up, turns left, steps left, and then turns right again. That pattern is called a loop; it's a set of commands the robot does several times the exact same way. When we find loops in our coding, we can write it like this 5(; that tells our robot to do repeat those commands five times before moving on to something new. Let's try this out by writing new code containing a loop and then having our robot act it out.

Appendix C

Are You in a Bubble?

Appendix D

Types of Nos

In today's society we like to be able to say yes to everything, but sometimes we forget that it's okay to say no. Here are some important ways to say no. As a group, discuss when/where you would use these different types of Nos.

1. **No, I need more time**. Sometimes we get overwhelmed by the different tasks in front of us. It is okay to say no because we need more time to complete the tasks that we are already working on.
2. **No, I am not interested in doing that**. If you are offered an activity that you really don't want to participate in, it is okay to communicate that you are not interested in that activity.
3. **No, I am sorry, but I already have something that day. Can we try another day?** Don't feel you have to reschedule or change something just because a friend had a different plan. This type of soft no allows you to work together to find a solution.
4. **No, I need help**. Sometimes we get overwhelmed because we don't have the skills/time to complete a task by ourselves. It is healthy to admit that we need some help to finish these types of goals.
5. **Stop. That is not safe!** If someone ever makes you feel unsafe it is important to communicate that using a hard no. When you use this no, make sure that you stand your ground and don't let the person push you around.

Appendix E

Sleep Plan Worksheet

Whether you want to put your best foot forward in class or maximize your focus playing through a video game, having a plan to make the most of your sleep can make a big difference. In this activity you will come up with a plan that will help you go to sleep quickly and wake up alert.

Bedtime		Wake Up	
T-2 Hours		Wake Up	
T-1 Hour		T 10 Min	
T-30 Min		T 30 Min	
T-10 Min		T 1 Hour	
Bedtime		T 2 Hours	

Appendix F

Creating Safe Passwords

A passphrase is an easy-to-remember word that makes a more secure password.

1. Pick a number: ____
2. Pick a technobabble term: __________________________________
3. Pick a phrase: ____
   ____
4. Abbreviate a phrase: ______________________________________
5. Replace letters: ____
6. Use core wording: ____

You now have all the information that you need to create the keys to your own content. Take a moment and think of one password that you would like to change today to improve your personal security.

Appendix G

Emoji Life Story Worksheet

My favorite memory of being with my family was:

When I grow up, I want to:

Appendix H

Digital Citizenship Coloring Page

References

Advocates for Youth. "Peer Programs: Looking at the Evidence of Effectiveness—a Literature Review." http://www.advocatesforyouth.org/publications/publications-a-z/1856-peer-programs-looking-at-the-evidence-of-effectiveness-a-literature-review. Accessed September 15, 2018.

Ahmad, Irfan. "Social Media Trends in 2018 [Infographic]." *Social Media Today*, February 15, 2018. Accessed April 20, 2018. https://www.socialmediatoday.com/news/social-media-trends-in-2018-infographic/517131/.

Aldrich, Clark. *Unschooling Rules: 55 Ways to Unlearn What We Know about Schools and Rediscover Education*. Austin, TX: Greenleaf, 2011.

American Pediatrics Association. "Media Use by Children Younger Than 2 Years." *Pediatrics* 128, no. 5 (2018). Accessed October 21, 2018. http://pediatrics.aappublications.org/content/128/5/1040.

Anderman, Eric M., and Lynley H. Anderman. "Egocentrism." In *Psychology of Classroom Learning: An Encyclopedia*, 1: 355–57. Farmington Hills, MI: Gale Cengage, 2009.

Anderson, Janna, and Lee Rainie. "The Future of Well-Being in a Tech-Saturated World." Pew Research Center, April 17, 2018. https://www.pewinternet.org/2018/04/17/the-future-of-well-being-in-a-tech-saturated-world/.

Anderson, Monica, and John B. Horrigan. "Smartphones Help Those without Broadband Get Online, but Don't Necessarily Bridge the Digital Divide." Pew Research Center, Fact Tank. Accessed August 19, 2018. http://www.pewresearch.org/fact-tank/2016/10/03/smartphones-help-those-without-broadband-get-online-but-dont-necessarily-bridge-the-digital-divide/.

Anderson, Monica, and Jingjing Jiang. "Teens, Social Media and Technology." Pew Research Center, May 31, 2018. Accessed October 10, 2018. http://www.pewinternet.org/2018/05/31/teens-social-media-technology-2018/.

Anderson, Monica, and Andrew Perrin. "Nearly One-in-Five Teens Can't Always Finish Their Homework Because of the Digital Divide." Pew Research Center, October 26, 2018. Accessed December 30, 2018. http://www.pewresearch.org/fact-tank/2018/10/26/nearly-one-in-five-teens-cant-always-finish-their-homework-because-of-the-digital-divide/.

Arky, Beth. "Choosing a Parent Training Program." Child Mind Institute. https://childmind.org/article/choosing-a-parent-training-program/.

ATT Internet Service. "Mbps vs. MBps: What's the Difference?" Accessed December 30, 2018. https://www.attinternetservice.com/resources/mbps-vs-mbps/.

Bandura, Albert. "Self-Efficacy Mechanism in Human Agency." *American Psychologist* 37, no. 2 (1982): 122–47. doi:10.1037/0003-066X.37.2.122.

Barlińska, Julia, Anna Szuster, and Mikołaj Winiewski. "Cyberbullying among Adolescent Bystanders: Role of Affective versus Cognitive Empathy in Increasing Prosocial Cyberbystander Behavior." *Frontiers in Psychology* 9 (May 2018): 799. doi: 10.3389/fpsyg.2018.00799.

Bashir, Saad. "Digital Equity." Seattle Information Technology. Accessed August 19, 2018. http://www.seattle.gov/tech/initiatives/digital-equity.

Bhardwaj, Prachi, and Shayanne Gal. "Siri Owns 46% of the Mobile Voice Assistant Market—One and a Half Times Google Assistant's Share of the Market." *Business Insider*, June 29, 2018. Accessed November 17, 2018. https://www.businessinsider.com/siri-google-assistant-voice-market-share-charts-2018-6.

Bowles, Nellie. "Silicon Valley Nannies Are Phone Police for Children." *New York Times*, October 26, 2018. Accessed December 10, 2018. https://www.nytimes.com/2018/10/26/style/silicon-valley-nannies.html?action=click&module=RelatedLinks&pgtype=Article.

———. "The Digital Gap between Rich and Poor Is Not What You Think." *New York Times*, October 26, 2018. Accessed December 10, 2018. https://www.nytimes.com/2018/10/26/style/digital-divide-screens-schools.html.

Brewer, G., and J. Kerslake. "Cyberbullying, Self-Esteem, Empathy and Loneliness." *Computers in Human Behavior* 48 (July 2015): 255–60. https://www.sciencedirect.com/science/article/pii/S0747563215001016.

BroadbandNow. "Fiber-Optic Internet in the United States." https://broadbandnow.com/Fiber. Accessed December 30, 2018.

Bureau of Labor Statistics. "Computer Ownership Up Sharply in the 1990s." *TED: The Economics Daily*. April 5, 1999. Accessed September 27, 2018. https://www.bls.gov/opub/ted/1999/Apr/wk1/art01.htm.

Burke, Kenneth. "How Many Texts Do People Send per Day (2018)?" *Text Request* (blog). Accessed November 9, 2018. https://www.textrequest.com/blog/how-many-texts-people-send-per-day/.

Carroll, Aaron E., and Austin Frakt. "It Saves Lives. It Can Save Money. So Why Aren't We Spending More on Public Health." *New York Times*, May 28, 2018. https://www.nytimes.com/2018/05/28/upshot/it-saves-lives-it-can-save-money-so-why-arent-we-spending-more-on-public-health.html.

CASEL. "CASEL Program Guides: Effective Social and Emotional Learning Programs." Accessed July 3, 2018. https://casel.org/guide/.

Centers for Disease Control and Prevention. "Sexual Violence: Risk and Protective Factors." Accessed November 21, 2018. https://www.cdc.gov/violenceprevention/sexualviolence/riskprotectivefactors.html.

———. "Suicide: Risk and Protective Factors." Accessed November 21, 2018.https://www.cdc.gov/violenceprevention/suicide/riskprotectivefactors.html.

———. "Violence: Risk and Protective Factors." Accessed November 21, 2018. https://www.cdc.gov/violenceprevention/youthviolence/riskprotectivefactors.html.

———. "Youth Risk Behavior Surveillance—United States, 2017." *Morbidity and Mortality Weekly Report*, June 15, 2008. https://www.cdc.gov/healthyyouth/data/yrbs/pdf/2017/ss6708.pdf.

Chalk, Andy. "US Lawmaker Who Called Out Star Wars Battlefront 2 Lays Out Plans for Anti-loot Box Law." *PC Gamer*, December 6, 2017. Accessed December 21, 2018. https://www.pcgamer.com/us-lawmaker-who-called-out-star-wars-battlefront-2-lays-out-plans-for-anti-loot-box-law/.

Champlain College. "Is Your State Making the Grade? 2017 National Report Card on State Efforts to Improve Financial Literacy in High School." Accessed December 21, 2018. https://www.champlain.edu/centers-of-experience/center-for-financial-literacy/report-national-high-school-financial-literacy.

Chapman, Alan. "Mehrabian's Communication Theory: Verbal, Non-verbal, Body Language." BusinessBalls. http://www.businessballs.com/mehrabiancommunications.htm.

Chatterjee, Rhitu. "More Screen Time for Teens Linked to ADHD Symptoms." NPR, July 17, 2018. Accessed October 21, 2018. https://www.npr.org/sections/health-shots/2018/07/17/629517464/more-screen-time-for-teens-may-fuel-adhd-symptoms.

Clark, J. L., S. B. Algoe, and M. C. Green. "Social Network Sites and Well-Being: The Role of Social Connection." *Current Directions in Psychological Science* 27, no. 1 (2018): 32–37. https://doi.org/10.1177/0963721417730833.

Clayton, Victoria. "The Psychological Approach to Educating Kids." *Atlantic*, March 30, 2017. Accessed July 3, 2018. https://www.theatlantic.com/education/archive/2017/03/the-social-emotional-learning-effect/521220/.

Common Sense Media. *Social Media, Social Life: How Teens View Their Digital Lives*. Accessed January 2, 2019. San Francisco: Common Sense Media, June 26, 2012. https://www.commonsensemedia.org/research/social-media-social-life-how-teens-view-their-digital-lives.

Connolly, Jennifer, Wendy Josephson, Jessica Schnoll, Emily Simkins-Strong, Debra Pepler, Alison MacPherson, Jessica Weiser, Michelle Moran, and Depeng Jiang. "Evaluation of a Youth-Led Program for Preventing Bullying, Sexual Harassment, and Dating Aggression in Middle Schools." *Journal of Early Adolescence* 35, no. 3 (2014): 403–34. https://doi.org/10.1177/0272431614535090.

Cook, Sam. "The First Amendment and What It Means for Free Speech Online." *Comparitech* (blog), February 10, 2017. https://www.comparitech.com/blog/vpn-privacy/the-first-amendment-what-it-means-free-speech-online/#gref.

Davis, Daphne, and Jeffrey A. Hayes. "What Are the Benefits of Mindfulness?" *Monitor on Psychology* 43, no. 7 (July–August 2012). Accessed December 15, 2018. https://www.apa.org/monitor/2012/07-08/ce-corner.aspx.

Deuze, M. "Participation, Remediation, Bricolage: Considering Principal Components of a Digital Culture." *Information Society* 22, no. 2 (2006): 63–75. doi:10.1080/01972240600567170.

Digital Citizenship Summit. "What Is a DigCit Summit?" Accessed August 19, 2018. http://digcitinstitute.com/digcitsummit/.

Dogtiev, Artyom. "App Download and Usage Statistics (2018)." Business of Apps, February 16, 2019. Accessed October 10. 2018. http://www.businessofapps.com/data/app-statistics/.

Duggan, Maeve. "Online Harassment 2017." Pew Research Center, July 11, 2017. http://www.pewinternet.org/2017/07/11/online-harassment-2017/.

Duncan, Eric. "Topic: E-commerce Worldwide." Statista. Accessed December 21, 2018. https://www.statista.com/topics/871/online-shopping/.

Etherington, Darrell. "Mobile Internet Use Passes Desktop Use for the First Time." *TechCrunch*, November 1, 2016. Accessed October 10, 2018. https://techcrunch.com/2016/11/01/mobile-internet-use-passes-desktop-for-the-first-time-study-finds/.

Federal Communications Commission. *2018 Broadband Deployment Report*. Washington, DC: FCC, February 2, 2018. Accessed December 30, 2018. https://www.fcc.gov/reports-research/reports/broadband-progress-reports/2018-broadband-deployment-report.

First Star Academy, University of Utah. "What Is First Star?" Accessed July 1, 2018. https://engagement.utah.edu/firststar/.

Fitzpatrick, Sally, and Kay Bussey. "The Role of Perceived Friendship Self-Efficacy as a Protective Factor against the Negative Effects of Social Victimization." *Social Development* 23, no. 1 (2013): 41–60. https://doi.org/10.1111/sode.12032.

Forrest, Connor. "Why an Internet 'Bill of Rights' Will Never Work, and What's More Important." *Tech Republic*, March 13, 2014. Accessed December 22, 2018. https://www.techrepublic.com/article/why-an-internet-bill-of-rights-will-never-work-and-whats-more-important/.

Fruja Amthor, R., and K. Roxas. "Multicultural Education and Newcomer Youth: Re-Imagining a More Inclusive Vision for Immigrant and Refugee Students." *Educational Studies* 52, no. 2 (2016): 155–76. https://doi.org/10.1080/00131946.2016.1142992.

Google. "On the 25th Anniversary of the Web Let's Keep It Free and Open." Google (official blog), March 11, 2014. Accessed December 22, 2018. https://googleblog.blogspot.com/2014/03/on-25th-anniversary-of-web-lets-keep-it.html.

Grieve, R., M. Indian, K. Witteveen, G. A. Tolan, and J. Marrington. "Face-to-Face or Facebook: Can Social Connectedness Be Derived Online?" *Computers in Human Behavior* 29, no. 3 (2013): 604–9.

Guardian. "Cutting-Edge Theatre: World's First Virtual Reality Operation Goes Live." *The Guardian*, April 14, 2016. Accessed October 15, 2018. https://www.theguardian.com/technology/2016/apr/14/cutting-edge-theatre-worlds-first-virtual-reality-operation-goes-live.

Hamari, Juho, Harri Sarsa, and Jonna Koivisto. "Does Gamification Work? A Literature Review of Empirical Studies on Gamification." Paper presented at the 47th Hawaii International Conference on System Sciences, 2014. Accessed May 4, 2018. https://ieeexplore.ieee.org/stamp/stamp.jsp?tp=&arnumber=6758978&isnumber=6758592.

Harari, Yuval Noh. "Why Technology Favors Tyranny." *Atlantic*, October 2018. Accessed November 24, 2018. https://www.theatlantic.com/magazine/archive/2018/10/yuval-noah-harari-technology-tyranny/568330/.

Hertz, Marcie Feldman, and Corinne David-Ferdon. *Electronic Media and Youth Violence: CDC Issue Brief for Educators and Caregivers*. Atlanta, GA: Centers for Disease Control, 2008. Accessed July 2, 2018. https://www.cdc.gov/violenceprevention/pdf/ea-brief-a.pdf.

Hertzog, J. L., T. Harpel, and R. Rowley. "Is It Bullying, Teen Dating Violence, or Both? Student, School Staff, and Parent Perceptions." *Children & Schools* 38, no. 1 (2016): 21–29.

ICanHelp. "Our Vision: Support Educators, Empower Students." Accessed September 15, 2018. https://www.icanhelpdeletenegativity.org/about/.

International Society for Technology in Education. "Digital Citizenship." Accessed August 19, 2018. https://www.iste.org/explore/category/digital-citizenship.

———. "Technology Foundation Standards for Students." Accessed August 19, 2018. http://www.iste.org/docs/pdfs/nets_for_students_1998_standards.pdf?sfvrsn=2.

Jacobson, M., and M. Ruddy. *Open to Outcome*. Oklahoma City, OK: Wood N Barnes.

Kludt, Tom, "Alex Jones' Bid to Throw Out Sandy Hook Defamation Lawsuit Denied." *CNN Business*, August 31, 2018. Accessed December 22, 2018. https://money.cnn.com/2018/08/30/media/alex-jones-pozner-defamation-suit/index.html.

Kolb, David A. *Experiential Learning: Experience as the Source of Learning and Development*. Upper Saddle River, NJ: Prentice-Hall, 1983.

Kruger, J., N. Epley, J. Parker, and Z.-W. Ng, "Egocentrism over E-mail: Can We Communicate as Well as We Think?" *Journal of Personality and Social Psychology* 89, no. 6 (2005): 925–36.

Leder, Jane Mersky. *Dead Serious: Breaking the Cycle of Teen Suicide*. 2nd edition. Self-published, 2018.

Leskin, Paige. "The 21 Scariest Data Breaches of 2018." *Business Insider*, December 30, 2018. Accessed December 22, 2018. https://www.businessinsider.com/data-hacks-breaches-biggest-of-2018-2018-12#2-marriott-starwood-hotels-500-million-20.

Levenson, J. C., A. Shensa, J. E. Sidani, J. B. Colditz, and B. A. Primack. "The Association between Social Media Use and Sleep Disturbance among Young Adults." *Preventive Medicine* 85, 36–41. Accessed October 21, 2018. http://doi.org/10.1016/j.ypmed.2016.01.001.

Levski, Yariv. "7 Virtual Reality Trends We're Predicting for 2018." *App Real* (blog). Accessed October 15, 2018. https://appreal-vr.com/blog/virtual-reality-trends/.

Lilienfeld, Scott O., and Hal Arkowitz. "Why 'Just Say No' Doesn't Work." *Scientific American*, January 1, 2014. Accessed July 2, 2018. https://www.scientificamerican.com/article/why-just-say-no-doesnt-work/.

Lorenz, Taylor. "Teens Explain the World of Snapchat's Addictive Streaks, Where Friendships Live or Die." *Business Insider*, April, 2017. Accessed September 3, 2018. https://www.businessinsider.com/teens-explain-snapchat-streaks-why-theyre-so-addictive-and-important-to-friendships-2017-4.

———. "Unidentified Plane-Bae Woman's Statement Confirms the Worst." *Atlantic*, July, 2018. Accessed November 17, 2018. https://www.theatlantic.com/technology/archive/2018/07/unidentified-plane-bae-womans-statement-confirms-the-worst/565139/.

Mac, Ryan. "Literally Just a Big List of Facebook's 2018 Scandals." Accessed December 22, 2018. https://www.buzzfeednews.com/article/ryanmac/literally-just-a-big-list-of-facebooks-2018-scandals.

Madden, Mary, Amanda Lenhart, Sandra Cortesi, Urs Gasser, Maeve Duggan, Aaron Smith, and Meredith Beaton. "Teens, Social Media, and Privacy." Pew Research Center, May 21, 2013. Accessed December 22, 2018. http://www.pewinternet.org/2013/05/21/teens-social-media-and-privacy/.

Madrigal, Alexis C. "Raised by YouTube." *Atlantic*, November 2018. Accessed October 21, 2018. https://www.theatlantic.com/magazine/archive/2018/11/raised-by-youtube/570838/.

Marcus, M. T., and A. Zgierska. "Mindfulness-Based Therapies for Substance Use Disorders: Part 1." *Substance Abuse* 30, no. 4 (2009): 263–65.

Matney, Lucas. "Virtual Reality Looks to Its Adolescence." *TechCrunch*, September 29, 2016. https://techcrunch.com/2016/09/29/virtual-reality-looks-to-its-adolescence/.

McCoy, Bernard. "Digital Distractions in the Classroom: Student Classroom Use of Digital Devices for Non-Class Related Purposes." *Faculty Publications, College of Journalism & Mass Communications* 71 (October 15, 2013).

McKenzie, Lindsay. "An Unending Copyright Dispute." *Inside Higher Ed*, October 30, 2018. Accessed December 20, 2018. https://www.insidehighered.com/news/2018/10/30/georgia-state-and-publishers-continue-legal-battle-over-fair-use-course-materials.

Mediakix. "The Mobile Gaming Industry: Statistics, Revenue, Demographics, More." Accessed October 10, 2018. http://mediakix.com/2018/03/mobile-gaming-industry-statistics-market-revenue/#gs.ipdCeKs.

Mehrabian, A., and S. R. Ferris. "Inference of Attitudes from Nonverbal Communication in Two Channels." *Journal of Consulting Psychology* 31, no. 3 (1967): 248–58.

Mehrabian, A., and M. Weiner. "Decoding of Inconsistent Communications." *Journal of Personality and Social Psychology* 6, no. 1 (1967): 109–14.

Merchant, Brian. *The One Device: The Secret History of the iPhone*. New York: Little, Brown, 2017.

Mishna, Faye, Charlene Cook, Tahany Gadalla, Joanne Daciuk, and Steven Solomon. "Cyber Bullying Behaviors among Middle and High School Students." *American Journal of Orthopsychiatry* 80, no. 3 (2010): 362–74.

Mossberger, Karen, Caroline J. Tolbert, and Ramona S. McNeal. *Digital Citizenship: The Internet, Society, and Participation*. Cambridge, MA: MIT Press, 2008.

Mueller, Daniel, and Amber Morczek. "Internet Pornography: Normalizing the Relationship between Violence and Sex." Presentation at the Utah Coalition against Sexual Assault, January 2018, Salt Lake City.

National Alliance to End Homelessness. "Foster Youth and Homelessness: What Are the Risk Factors?" NAEH. https://endhomelessness.org/foster-kids-and-homelessness-what-are-the-risk-factors/.

National Sleep Foundation. "Teens and Sleep." Accessed July 3, 2018. https://sleepfoundation.org/sleep-topics/teens-and-sleep.

Neiger, Chris. "Facebook Doubles Down on Virtual Reality." *Motley Fool*, May 13, 2018. Accessed October 15, 2018. https://www.fool.com/investing/2018/05/13/facebook-doubles-down-on-virtual-reality.aspx.

Nurse-Family Partnership. "About Us." Accessed July 2, 2018 https://www.nursefamilypartnership.org/about/.

Okpych, N. J., and M. E. Courtney. "Characteristics of Foster Care History as Risk Factors for Psychiatric Disorders among Youth in Care." *American Journal of Orthopsychiatry* 88, no. 3 (2018): 269–81. https://www.ncbi.nlm.nih.gov/pubmed/28253015.

Pagnoni, G. "Dynamical Properties of BOLD Activity from the Ventral Posteromedial Cortex Associated with Meditation and Attentional Skills." *Journal of Neuroscience* 32, no. 15 (2012): 5242–49.

Parents as Teachers. "What We Do." Accessed July 2, 2018. https://parentsasteachers.org/what-we-do/.

Payne, Ruby K., Philip DeVol, and Terie Dreussi Smith. *Bridges out of Poverty: Strategies for Professionals and Communities*. Highlands, TX: aha! Process.

Perez, Matt. Report: "Esports to Grow Substantially and Near Billion-Dollar Revenues in 2018." *Forbes*, February 21, 2018. https://www.forbes.com/sites/mattperez/2018/02/21/report-esports-to-grow-substantially-and-near-a-billion-dollar-revenues-in-2018/#dac91e52b019.

Perez, Sarah. "Voice-Enabled Smart Speakers to Reach 55% of U.S. Households by 2022, Says Report." *TechCrunch*, November 8, 2017. Accessed November 17, 2018. https://techcrunch.com/2017/11/08/voice-enabled-smart-speakers-to-reach-55-of-u-s-households-by-2022-says-report/.

Pew Research Center. "Mobile Fact Sheet." Pew Research Center, February 5, 2018. Accessed September 27, 2018. http://www.pewinternet.org/fact-sheet/mobile/.

Pierce, T. "Social Anxiety and Technology: Face-to-Face Communication versus Technological Communication among Teens." *Computers in Human Behavior* 25, no. 6 (2009): 1367–72.

Pillay, Srini. "The 'Thinking' Benefits of Doodling." *Harvard Health Blog*, December 15, 2016. Accessed December 14, 2018. https://www.health.harvard.edu/blog/the-thinking-benefits-of-doodling-2016121510844.

Poushter, Jacob, Caldwell Bishop, and Hanyi Chwe. "Smartphone Ownership on the Rise in Emerging Economies." Pew Research Center, June 19, 2018. Accessed November 17, 2018. http://www.pewglobal.org/2018/06/19/2-smartphone-ownership-on-the-rise-in-emerging-economies/.

Project Tomorrow. *Making Learning Mobile 3.0: The Double Bottom Line with Mobile Learning Closing the Homework Gap and Enhancing Student Achievement Results of the Project Evaluation Study*. McLean, VA: Kajeet. Accessed September 27, 2018. http://cdn2.hubspot.net/hubfs/367813/MLM3-Report.pdf?t=1496671066579.

"Psycho Dad Destroys Xbox." Accessed July 1, 2018. https://www.youtube.com/watch?reload=9&v=0AUoJXh4Q6U.

Pulcini C. D., B. T. Zima, K. J. Kelleher, et al. "Poverty and Trends in Three Common Chronic Disorders." *Pediatrics* 139, no. 3 (2017): e20162539.

Ra, C. K., J. Cho, M. D. Stone, et al. "Association of Digital Media Use with Subsequent Symptoms of Attention-Deficit/Hyperactivity Disorder among Adolescents." *Journal of the American Medical Association* 320, no. 3 (2018): 255–63. doi:10.1001/jama.2018.8931.

Ribble, Mike. *Digital Citizenship in Schools*. Eugene, OR: International Society for Technology in Education, 2011.

———. "Essential Elements of Digital Citizenship." ISTE, June 25, 2014. https://www.iste.org/explore/ArticleDetail?articleid=101.

Rogers-Whitehead, Carrie. "Everything You Need to Know about the Deepfake Phenomenon." KSL, July 30, 2018. Accessed September 27, 2018. https://www.ksl.com/?sid=46368765&nid=1012&title=everything-you-need-to-know-about-the-deepfake-phenomenon.

———. "5 Tips to Help Your Kid Put Down the Screen and Go to Sleep." KSL, May 3, 2018. Accessed July 3, 2018. https://www.ksl.com/article/46313498/5-tips-to-help-your-kid-put-down-the-screen-and-go-to-sleep.

———. "4 Social Media Scams That Could Cost You," KSL, August 23. 2017. https://www.ksl.com/?sid=45523403&nid=1012.

———. "4 Things to Know about Teaching Digital Literacy to Refugees." ISTE, June 4, 2018. Accessed December 29, 2018. https://www.iste.org/explore/articleDetail?articleid=2209.

———. "Here's What You Need to Know about Cyberbullying." KSL. October 16, 2018. Accessed November 21, 2018. https://www.ksl.com/article/46407726/heres-what-you-need-to-know-about-cyberbullying.

———. "How SLC Is Tackling the Issue of 'Digital Inclusion.'" KSL. Accessed August 19, 2018. https://www.ksl.com/?sid=39819066&nid=1012.

———. "Increasing Digital Inclusion in Utah." *Silicon Slopes*, May 10, 2017. Accessed August 19, 2018. https://medium.com/silicon-slopes/increasing-digital-inclusion-in-utah-b406b466d56c.

———. "Is WiGig the Answer to Faster WiFi?" KSL, November 14, 2016. Accessed October 12, 2018. https://www.ksl.com/?sid=42208599&nid=1012&title=is-wigig-the-answer-to-faster-wifi.

———. "Salt Lake City Commits to Forming Digital Inclusion Plan. Here's Why That Matters." KSL, November 16, 2018. Accessed December 30, 2018. https://www.ksl.com/

article/46428957/salt-lake-city-commits-to-forming-digital-inclusion-plan-heres-why-that-matters.

———. "The Discord with Discord: What Parents Need to Know about the Popular Gamer Chat." KSL, December 5, 2018. Accessed December 22, 2018. https://www.ksl.com/?nid=968&sid=46441334.

———. "Use Venmo? Apple Pay? Watch Out for These 3 Mobile Payment Pitfalls." KSL, June 5, 2018. Accessed December 20, 2018. https://www.ksl.com/article/46335017/use-venmo-apple-pay-watch-out-for-these-3-mobile-payment-pitfalls.

———. "Utah Ranked 11th for Internet Connection, Works to Expand Digital Inclusion." KSL, May 8, 2017. Accessed September 27, 2018. https://www.ksl.com/?nid=1012&sid=44168481.

———. "What Is the Homework Gap? How Digital Inclusion Affects Your Students." *Utah Afterschool Network* (blog), July 10, 2017. Accessed September 27, 2018. https://utahafterschool.org/utah-afterschool-blog/item/49-what-is-the-homework-gap-how-digital-inclusion-affects-your-students.

———. "What Hip, New App Are the Kids Using These Days? TikTok." KSL, September 24, 2018. Accessed January 1, 2019. https://www.ksl.com/article/46395869/what-hip-new-app-are-the-kids-using-these-days-tiktok.

Rose, Chad A., Amanda B. Nickerson, and Melissa Stormont. "Advancing Bullying Research from a Social-Ecological Lens: An Introduction to the Special Issue." *School Psychology Review* 44, no. 4 (2015).

Rovell, Darren. "427 Million People Will Be Watching Esports by 2019, Reports Newzoo." *ESPN.com*, May 11, 2016. Accessed October 14, 2018. http://www.mindshareintheloop.com/home/2016/06/14/game-on-what-marketers-should-know-about-esports-fans/.

Ryan, Camille. "Computer and Internet Use in the United States: 2016." US Census Bureau, August 8, 2018. Accessed September 27, 2018. https://www.census.gov/library/publications/2018/acs/acs-39.html.

SAMHSA. "Trauma and Violence." US Department of Health and Human Services. Accessed July 2, 2018. https://www.samhsa.gov/trauma-violence/types.

School-Based Health Alliance. "Youth Participation Models." Accessed September 15, 2018. http://www.sbh4all.org/training/youth-development/youth-engagement-toolkit/youth-participation-models/.

Schrader, P. G., and Kimberly A. Lawless. "The Knowledge, Attitudes, and Behaviors Approach How to Evaluate Performance and Learning in Complex Environments." *Performance Improvement* 43, no. 9 (2004): 8–15.

Sentance, Rebecca. "The State of Mobile Voice Search in 2018." Econsultancy, July 12, 2018. Accessed October 10, 2018. https://econsultancy.com/the-state-of-mobile-voice-search-in-2018/.

SEO Hacker. "Lesson #28: How Important Is It to Be on the First Page of SERPs?" SEO Hacker. March 22, 2019. Accessed October 10, 2018. https://seo-hacker.com/lesson-28-important-page-serps/.

Shahbaz, Adrian. *Freedom on the Net 2018: The Rise of Digital Authoritarianism*. Washington, DC: Freedom House. Accessed January 1, 2019. https://freedomhouse.org/report/freedom-net/freedom-net-2018.

Siefer, Angela. "Worst Connected Cities 2016." National Digital Inclusion Alliance (blog), June 7, 2018. Accessed September 27, 2018. https://www.digitalinclusion.org/blog/2018/06/07/worst-connected-cities-2016/.

Smith, Aaron. "Record Shares of Americans Now Own Smartphones, Have Home Broadband." Pew Research Center, January 12, 2017. Accessed November 17, 2019. http://www.pewresearch.org/fact-tank/2017/01/12/evolution-of-technology/.

Smith, Aaron, and Monica Anderson. "Social Media in Use 2018, Appendix A: Detailed Table." Pew Research Center, March 1, 2018. Accessed January 1, 2019. http://www.pewinternet.org/2018/03/01/social-media-use-2018-appendix-a-detailed-table/.

Snopes. "Was the Sandy Hook Elementary School Shooting a Hoax?" Accessed December 22, 2018. https://www.snopes.com/fact-check/sandy-hook-exposed/.

Statista. "Age Breakdown of Video Game Players in the United States in 2018." Accessed October 10, 2018. https://www.statista.com/statistics/189582/age-of-us-video-game-players-since-2010/.

———. "Number of Mobile App Downloads Worldwide in 2017, 2018 and 2022, by Region (in billions)." Accessed October 10, 2018. https://www.statista.com/statistics/266488/forecast-of-mobile-app-downloads/.

Strohmeyer, Robert. "The 7 Worst Tech Predictions of All Time." *Infoworld*, January 5, 2009. Accessed September 27, 2018. https://www.infoworld.com/article/2675265/security/the-7-worst-tech-predictions-of-all-time.html.

Taren, A. A., J. D. Creswell, and P. J. Gianaros. "Dispositional Mindfulness Co-Varies with Smaller Amygdala and Caudate Volumes in Community Adults." *PLoS ONE* 8, no. 5 (2013): e64574. https://doi.org/10.1371/journal.pone.0064574.

Thorn. "Sextortion." Accessed November 29, 2018. https://www.stopsextortion.com.

Turati, C., F. Simion, I. Milani, and C. Umiltà. "Newborns' Preference for Faces: What Is Crucial?" *Developmental Psychology* 38, no. 6 (2002): 875–82.

US Bank. "Digital Payment Platforms Primed to Topple Cash." August 16, 2017. Accessed December 20, 2018. https://www.usbank.com/newsroom/news/digital-payment-platforms-primed-to-topple-cash.html.

US Department of Health and Human Services. *AFCARS Report*. Accessed July 2, 2018. https://www.acf.hhs.gov/sites/default/files/cb/afcarsreport24.pdf.

US Securities and Exchange Commission. "Beware of Pyramid Schemes Posing as Multi-Level Marketing Programs." October 1, 2013. Accessed December 21, 2018. https://www.sec.gov/oiea/investor-alerts-bulletins/investor-alerts-ia_pyramidhtm.html.

Utah Department of Health. "Utah Health Status Update: CDC Investigation Shows Youth Suicides in Utah Increasing." December 2017. Accessed November 27, 2018. https://health.utah.gov/vipp/pdf/Suicide/HealthStatusUpdateCDCEpi-AidYouthSuicide.pdf.

Vanderwert, R. E., E. A. Simpson, A. Paukner, S. J. Suomi, N. A. Fox, and P. F. Ferrari. "Early Social Experience Affects Neural Activity to Affiliative Facial Gestures in Newborn Nonhuman Primates." *Developmental Neuroscience* 37, no. 3 (2015): 243–52.

Varner, J., K. Hoch, M. C. Goates, and C. Hanson. "Proactive Protection for Adolescents, the Innocent Victim: Risk and Protective Factors for Pornography." Presentation at the Utah Society of Public Health Educators Annual Conference, Ogden, Utah, September 2017.

Virtual Reality Society. "History of Virtual Reality." https://www.vrs.org.uk/virtual-reality/history.html.

Welch, K., and A. A. Payne. "Zero Tolerance School Policies." In *The Palgrave International Handbook of School Discipline, Surveillance, and Social Control*, edited by J. Deakin, E. Taylor, and A. Kupchik. Cham, Switzerland: Palgrave Macmillan.

White, Caitlin. "Public Shaming: When the Internet Never Forgets Is It Possible to Heal?" *Medium*, December 11, 2017. Accessed July 2, 2018. https://medium.com/s/digital-trauma/public-shaming-e9b0815d98fc.

White, S. W., D. Oswald, T. Ollendick, and L. Scahill. "Anxiety in Children and Adolescents with Autism Spectrum Disorders." *Clinical Psychology Review* 29, no. 3 (2009): 216–29. doi: 10.1016/j.cpr.2009.01.003. PMC 2692135.

Wijman, Tom. "New Gaming Boom: Newzoo Ups Its 2017 Global Games Market Estimate to $116.0Bn Growing to $143.5Bn in 2020." Newzoo, November 28, 2017. Accessed October 10, 2018. https://newzoo.com/insights/articles/new-gaming-boom-newzoo-ups-its-2017-global-games-market-estimate-to-116-0bn-growing-to-143-5bn-in-2020/.

Wilding, R. "Mediating Culture in Transnational Spaces: An Example of Young People from Refugee Backgrounds." *Continuum: Journal of Media & Cultural Studies* 26, no. 3 (2012): 501–11. https://doi.org/10.1080/10304312.2012.665843.

Wilkins, N., B. Tsao, M. Hertz, R. Davis, and J. Klevens. *Connecting the Dots: An Overview of the Links among Multiple Forms of Violence*. Atlanta, GA, and Oakland, CA: National Center for Injury Prevention and Control; Centers for Disease Control and Prevention; and Prevention Institute.

Wittes, Benjamin, Cody Poplin, Quinta Jurecic, and Clara Spera. *Sextortion: Cyber Security, Teenagers, and Remote Sexual Assault*. Washington, DC: Center for Technology Innovation at Brookings, May 2016. Accessed November 29, 2018. https://www.brookings.edu/wp-content/uploads/2016/05/sextortion1-1.pdf.

About the Author

Carrie Rogers-Whitehead is the founder of Digital Respons-Ability, a mission-based company that works with educators, students, and parents on the subject of digital citizenship. They have trained hundreds of K–12 students and offer professional and continuing education CEUs to educators who want to teach digital citizenship.

Carrie is a former TEDx speaker and librarian. She also is an instructor with Salt Lake Community College and was chosen as one of *Utah Businesses*' "40 under 40" leaders. Carrie is passionate about research and writing about complicated tech and educational subjects for a general audience. She writes a digital parenting column for KSL News and is a regular contributor and blogger on tech to outlets such as the International Society for Technology in Education. Carrie is the author of *Teen Fandom and Geek Programming: A Practical Guide for Librarians* (Rowman & Littlefield, 2018), and regularly trains and consults with libraries.

Carrie lives in Utah with her husband and son. While she enjoys teaching and writing about tech, you'll typically find her surrounded by books, paper, and pen.